"I have not seen another nonfiction book that offers such a perceptive, engaging, intimate chronicle of the early 1970s, the road-weary hippie hitchhikers, the anti-war sentiment, the dope-induced haze. Boruch . . . captures this very specific, significant time and place with exquisite clarity and lyric detail and description."

DINTY MOORE, author of *Between Panic and Desire*

"Marianne takes off into the unknown with $10, carrying her begging bowl and having the artist's faith that it will be filled with story. She never questions it. She's curious, and she follows that curiosity. The universe doesn't disappoint."

SUSAN NEVILLE, author of *Sailing the Inland Sea*

"From its first page *The Glimpse Traveler* launches us on a trajectory—an *On The Road*–style westward-ho picaresque journey through 1971 American culture—Berkeley, Big Sur, Esalen, communes galore, and even normality, in all its strangeness. Marianne Boruch is a bona-fide story teller, and the episodes are unobtrusively salted with the narrator's curious, wry, deeply intelligent, and lyrical meditations about love, selves, art, beauty, and knowability. *The Glimpse Traveler* is a wise, vulnerable, perfectly configured piece of literature, and a great read as well."

TONY HOAGLAND

"*The Glimpse Traveler* is a wild romp into the wild romp of the 1971, trippy, establishment-hating past, with all the accoutrements: hitchhiking, hippie vans, communes, Esalen, nude sun-bathing, hot-tubbing, bong-hitting— you name it, Marianne Boruch has got it covered. Hilarious satire, tender coming-of-age-making-of-a-poet memoir, bursting with dazzling language and marvelous characters. A stunning book!"

KAREN BRENNAN, author of *Being With Rachel*

the glimpse traveler

MARIANNE BORUCH

INDIANA UNIVERSITY PRESS

Bloomington & Indianapolis

This book is a publication of

Indiana University Press
601 North Morton Street
Bloomington, Indiana 47404–3797 USA

iupress.indiana.edu

Telephone orders   800-842-6796
Fax orders   812-855-7931
Orders by e-mail   iuporder@indiana.edu

♾ The paper used in this publication
meets the minimum requirements of
the American National Standard for
Information Sciences—Permanence
of Paper for Printed Library Materials,
ANSI Z39.48–1992.
Manufactured in the United States of
America

Library of Congress Cataloging-in-
Publication Data

Boruch, Marianne, 1950–
The glimpse traveler / Marianne Boruch.
p. cm. — (Break away books)
ISBN 978-0-253-22344-9
(pbk. : alk. paper)
ISBN 978-0-253-00555-7 (e-book)
1. Boruch, Marianne, 1950– I. Title.
PS3552.O75645Z46   2011
811'.54—dc23   2011025354
[B]

1 2 3 4 5 16 15 14 13 12 11

Again, in memory of
Elinor Brogden—wild and rare spirit.

We are all pilgrims and strangers.

—HANS BARTH
1876–1928

from his gravestone near Keats,
both buried in Rome

the glimpse traveler

There's rain and there's rain. Maybe there's a difference at the edge of a continent. Late afternoon when we entered the cabin. I didn't know the guy. A friend of a friend of a friend bent over the old phonograph—a record player we called them as kids, small and nearly square, with dull silver buckles, a plastic handle, worn leatherette skin. The kind you lower the arm and bring the needle down yourself. Like sparking a flame, that quick broken note before it takes and follows the groove of the record, into music.

We stood and listened to him listening. I have no idea: jazz or a slow ballad, some rock star burning out in a year or two. So many scratches, the wash of static, the rain outside. How the ear gets past all that, and surrenders. Or his hunger, so deeply tangled. Had I ever seen such pleasure? The moment just before, how it really sounded.

I was 20, traveling into glimpses. No matter what, he said, you have to hear it.

1

No plan that Thursday but a big breakfast—eggs, toast. The classic college boyfriend's apartment: milling about and underfoot, one or two other boys and their maybe girls. A straggly neighbor born *Harold,* called *Chug,* forever turning up to make a point then stopping mid-sentence. Someone's cousin crashed there for week. Someone's half-sister from Cincinnati figuring out her life. Not to mention the dog, the cat, and nothing picked up off the floor, no sink or toilet cleaned in how long. Books read and loved and passed on, dope smoked or on a windowsill, nesting in a small plastic bag. Jokes bad and repeated, *nice talking to ya,* we'd say to end any blowhard's rant, laughing.

Then my boyfriend Jack, at the stove, frying potatoes, onions for omelets: meet Frances, she's the one—I told you—hitchhiking west. Day after tomorrow. Early Saturday, right Frances? For a week or so. Then coming back.

She turned to me, this stranger: hey, want to go?

What? Was it a thought before I said it? No, my yes. Which—in the parlance of the day—was a shrug and a *sure.*

Almost spring, 1971. I couldn't look her in the eye.

2

What I took:

Ten bucks.

Two blank checks, folded down to razorblade dimensions. I
had a whopping $200 or so, saved in the bank.

Two shirts, plus the black turtleneck I had on.

An extra pair of jeans, extra underwear, extra socks.

A toothbrush, toothpaste, deodorant, tampons, aspirin,
band-aids, a half roll of toilet paper, pushed down flat.

The skinniest towel in the world, soap, a comb, a brush.

One coat, which I wore. And shoes, thick canvas,
just sneakers really.

The beret on my head.

A small notebook, a pencil.

One blue sweater with wooden buttons and they closed or
they opened.

A metal canteen, its cap kept by a tiny silver chain, a drop of
solder on either end, its canvas darkened in places, damp,
or about to be.

Two apples, an orange, peanut butter, a pocket knife, a half
loaf of bread.

My good luck charm, a holy card, also folded unto its razorblade: St. Christopher, patron saint of travel, who held the

Christ child high on one shoulder, crossing a rather dangerous ribbon of water. He looked burdened in the picture, resolved but awkward with that globe of his in the other hand, that walking stick. Way too much to carry.

My University of Illinois ID, my driver's permit. The address and phone number of my mother, faraway elsewhere, peacefully oblivious, her usual state regarding my antics since she dropped me at my freshman dorm saying: *you're going to do things I never would—just don't tell me.* As for Jack—should I write down his number too? Did I really want him called by some cop, some hospital clerk? After all, this was for emergencies, a phone number they'd find *on* me.

A second good luck holy card, St. Anthony, patron saint of lost things, sweet dead-on finder of whatever—if you do your part, and look.

Gloves, one in each pocket.

A backpack, of course—army surplus, clearly a former life there, torn, the open places sewn into scars with black thread by somebody.

A book, though mainly in cars I'd be sleeping or staring or talking. Was it *Day of the Locust* or *My Antonia* or something by Knut Hamsun?—all Jack's picks; he said they were good, they were great.

And sunglasses, the cheapest kind, marked down, on sale: 39 cents. Because the light, Frances said. California light being famous, and fierce.

3

Jack had told me about her, about Frances. Just a year older than I was but at 21, married three years, a widow for eight months now, since the car crash in Colorado. She never even tried college—*are you nuts? Study that shit?* she'd said. She had a job somewhere. He wasn't sure exactly, something with children. Maybe a teacher's aide in a classroom. Or maybe some place for kids too young for school, but their parents worked all day. Jack knew her because he knew Ned.

Her husband, Ned. I remember seeing him around that small town, DeKalb, Illinois. Thick red hair grown out haywire. Certain guys could manage that, the curly-headed ones who refused haircuts, months into years. As was habit then. I guess you'd call him a hippie, capital H. If you saw him, you'd think that, *hippie,* no question, Ned at the far edge of that grid. More than the usual drugs. That was rumor. Yet here he was—*a husband.* Some retro moment in the-life-so-far had flooded his future. Dramatic, exotic in a twisted, Ward Cleaver sort of way: to be married, at our age. I couldn't imagine. Thus Frances, a wife at 17. But suddenly, thus *not.* After the crash, I mean. Ned-the-no-longer, Ned nevermore-to-be. And Frances, a young woman abruptly older by way of a story and a shadow, its weight each morning when she came to again from whatever she had dreamt, whoever she was in that place of dreams. Not that I could absorb any of it. Not that it was even my business.

It's weird that she asked you, Jack said early that evening.

I lived in Champaign, about three hours south, where I was in school. But I'd gotten a lift off the ride-board to Jack's, his town, his college, the place I'd transferred from a year or so earlier. My spring break had pretty much started. And now, of course, this sudden new idea, this *journey,* for that delicious blank slate of how many days. I'd never been anywhere west unless you counted a camp counselor job two summers before, one state over and up, in the Minnesota woods.

It got dark later, being March. Jack sat by the window, still visible in the day's thin light, trying to pick out one of those first Leo Kottke tunes on his old guitar. Then he had statistics to do, *The Great Gatsby* to read. His break was later.

This might be one of those blow-it-all-to-hell trips for her. You really want to sign on to that?

I guess I'll find out, I said.

4

So I had one day to get ready. You saw how I packed. But I told Frances: I know this guy.

And the guy was Woodrow Joseph Brookston, ex-boyfriend of my high school friend Alexandra—Crazy Alex for short—who was a student at the U of I too, her apartment three blocks from me. Back now, Woody had been in Champaign a couple of days, just released at last and for good, out of Vietnam. Not a soldier, I assured Frances. He was a CO, really. But they made him go anyway, as a medic for two years. From DeKalb I had called other friends near where I lived on Green Street. Woody was crashing on the couch at their place, sort of a refugee from the army and now, from Alex. He answered the phone so I told him about the trip.

A medic in 'Nam? Frances said with interest, even reverence. I could see the movie she started to run in her head: Woody hauling the wounded into trucks and helicopters, holding high the blood bottles; Woody with a big red cross on his arm, the soundtrack full of gunshot and moody cello with an occasional lightning hit of violin; Woody, some tall beefy thoughtful guy, the real hero over there, all the broken, bleeding, stoned-out soldiers grateful and weeping and getting him to write down their last words to mail home to their girlfriends, or maybe even deliver by hand, walking up the little steps to their houses, knocking fatefully on each door. And those guys would trust him absolutely *not* to put the moves on their girls, even after a properly pious interval of a week or two.

In fact, Woody was skinny, not much taller than I was. He had that cool name, and seemed good-natured. I mean he was pleasant enough. *Pleasant.* Maybe that was code.

Dullsville, Alex had told me. I mean it. You'd think he'd have something to say about this goddamn war at least, wouldn't you? Something intelligent?

Technically, it's not a war, I said.

Okay. That. But will you listen? Woody's gotten a hundred times worse. Hanging out with him? Like spending the day with a pile of drifting snow. No, really! There's zero zero zero life on that planet, she said, tapping the side of her head. Nada! She said it again, coming down with a hammer on both syllables: *Na-da.*

Dull is underrated, I said. There are too many smarty-pants, cool and groovy know-it-alls in the world as it is. They're all over the place. Maybe it just takes him a while. Anyway, Woody's a big reader, isn't he? He loves books.

Yawn, she said, nice try.

So I wasn't surprised when Crazy Alex dumped him. But he hadn't believed it, had hitchhiked to Champaign from the east coast somewhere after his discharge, just to find out for sure. For sure *now* he was stricken. Quiet-stricken. Woody wasn't into fireworks or self-pity. That was Alex's job. But he was an optimist. She still likes me, he kept saying. She said so.

We all like you, Woody, I said. That's not the point in these matters.

But Woody's parents had moved to Oregon the previous year. He was headed west too, now that the Alex thing appeared to be over. So he definitely came to when I mentioned the trip. Could he go with us? He would hitch up to DeKalb in a shot, no big deal.

I thought clearly for maybe ten seconds. A guy along could be a plus. Obviously, it would be safer than two women traveling alone. And in spite of Alex's ideas on the subject, I suspected Woody could be a talker, someone quite happy in the front seat, holding forth on baseball and dumb TV shows with any redneck driver. And the Vietnam business. A little iffy, that one, depending on who picked us up. His stupid army haircut, for instance, could send a message either way; it would take a while to grow out. But his having been a medic, that was good from any angle. And his CO, even better in some quarters. In any case, I imagined Frances and I could make it a habit, scrambling into the back seat to read or sleep, leaving the driver to Woody who would chat him up, mile after mile. Besides, he *was* a medic, for god's sake. What if one of us closed a hand in a car door? What if we got food poisoning or a rabid dog attacked us? I knew it wasn't up there with gunfire and Agent Orange but I could see him earnestly talking to any ambulance guy after the engine caught fire and blew up, knowing the medical lingo, the exact right way to lift us onto a stretcher.

The only bad thing was *three* of us. Every extra body decreased your chance of getting picked up on the road. That was a law of physics or something. And females were, in theory, not prone to mass murder the way a guy might be. So with Woody, we'd be scarier out there to the more timid sort of driver, nervous about doing a good deed. Still.

Frances listened to all this rather inscrutably. Actually, I was talking to her on the phone, from Jack's. I heard her take a sip of something, probably a Coke or maybe just water. I pictured her tossing back her long black hair. A curious silence then. I knew she was thinking through all the parts and gluing them together.

What the hell, she said. Tell him yes.

5

There are a boatload of ways to hitchhike. It was a minor art form back then, late '60s, early '70s. With a homemade block-lettered sign—*Cedar Rapids* or *Denver* or *Anywhere West.* Or no sign at all. That was the purist stance, the one I favored. A thumb out in a tentative, subtle way, or the whole arm practically waving if one got desperate. People worked up a method over time; that was inevitable because those trips could take days and days. More flamboyant travelers—depending on how bored they got—would do a little jig, get a leg into it, swinging out over the pavement, something goofy, a Busby Berkeley sort of number to get attention.

The fact is—everyone was on the road. And proof, those long lines of patient hitchhikers on most interstate ramps. The etiquette wasn't elaborate but it was firm: you queued up in order of arrival. You took your turn. Sometimes twenty people long, that line. So you stood at the end of it and watched as stopping cars swallowed your compatriots, those strangers, one by one, until you were up, you were next. It was important to look cheerful and innocent. Meaning: harmless. That was key. *Pathetic,* never a great choice though I knew it was possible, lying dormant in the mix whether you willed it or not. We decided on no sign.

Better to surprise them with how far we want to go *as* or even *after* we get in the car, Frances advised. *California* written out, up front, might scare them. Maybe they wouldn't want to be stuck that many miles and they'd realize how awkward it would be, kicking us out in the middle of Iowa, pretending hey, they just remembered, this was *it,* the farthest they'd be going. As she talked, I flashed on the truth of that: some guy slowing down on a whim, his staring, picturing the three of us in his car for so long—*oh, god, no!*—then speeding up, and past.

Woody thought that was okay, a good idea. Woody thought everything was okay. He was up for the trip. Right, he said, no sign. Bingo. Less to carry.

And those first rides, yet to come—all fairly easy at first though it was start and stop; we had to wait at times, up to an hour or so. There was the fellow selling insurance, right out of DeKalb, going south to LaSalle where we picked up route 80, a test case while Frances and I hunkered down in the backseat. Right off, Woody turned pro just as I predicted, a biz-magnet, an irresistible regular guy. The driver's name: John W. O'Connor Jr. He wore a tie and had three kids; he loved that TV show, *Bonanza,* Adam clearly the smartest Cartwright brother though he liked Hoss the best because he had a great big heart. A big heart is key, isn't it? he asked Woody in a deliberate kind of voice like he was Socrates, like this line of thinking might lead to a treatise or two.

At that Frances made a face and mouthed *Hoss,* her cheeks puffed out, Hoss being pretty porky, the largest of those three brothers. She was trying not to laugh.

John W. O'Connor Jr. sold for Allstate, the best company, hands down. I mean, if you're going to shell out for insurance. You do have insurance, don't you? he said to Woody.

So it would go. A series of short lifts through Illinois: Cheryl Bauer, the dental assistant who hated teeth, then Mr. Felix, a retired baseball coach and science teacher—the first Afro-American teacher in my district, he told us gravely—turned ping-pong fanatic and thinking about trying his hand at romance novels. Then Rod Ketchem, newly kicked out of his apartment in Peoria, on the move now. He seemed a little dodgy, kind of a greaseball. His girlfriend was still plenty, plenty pissed, he told us. No wonder, Frances and I agreed later. But there in the car, Woody, at least, was all sympathy. In short, the three of us settled in, getting the hang of it easily enough.

But Saturday morning, that kitchen in DeKalb before any of this came to life, Jack was making us cheese sandwiches, cheddar on rye. These bananas too, he said, and this box of Ritz crackers. You guys share these. Woody—here!—put this stuff in your pack.

6

It was still threatening winter. Snow, and then a thaw. A thaw, then snow. A little or a lot. That was March in the middle west. Coat, gloves, a hat: we kept them close through Illinois on venerable route 80, a road widened and pounded into place all the way to San Francisco, sometimes exactly where the old Lincoln Highway had been, which, in turn, cut through stretches where wagon train wheels had famously sunk into mud or creaked and rattled on. Before that, an old Indian and trapper trail.

Mark twain! the old steamboaters once yelled out—a good news thing, the depth of the water safe. I'd read that, and remembered again as we drove over the Mississippi at Rock Island, toward Davenport. Look! I said, lurching forward to shake Woody's shoulder, then sideways, grabbing Frances's arm. I pointed at the window, the amazing muddy expanse: Guys! Check it out! That's the freaking Mississippi River out there!

Woody was saying something to the driver about Cassius Clay–Muhammad Ali for a few years now. He didn't even look back at me. Frances scowled, annoyed at the interruption. She was trying to sleep.

Sell the banjo, would you? I could hear my brother telling me. *You're such a sucker for this cornball stuff.*

But we were crossing the greatest of all rivers I knew, the Mississippi of song and story, a passage without notice, with no astonishment at all. Shouldn't we be *seeing* this, making it an occasion? Not some dopey movie of a trip. This was *it,* so cheesy it was past cheesy.

We kept speeding west, Frances dozing on and off, Woody onto the next subject with Mr. Lutowski, our good-hearted driver, and the driver after that: what about Gene McCarthy, was he thinking about running again? was Ted Kennedy even an option now? wasn't *Laugh-In* about the best damn thing on the air?

Outside it would gradually turn to wheat and grazing land, to full-blown *prairie,* not simply land wrenched by sweat and axe from its woods. Because hadn't it had always been like this, endless and pretty much treeless? I knew those fields would eventually *give way,* rolling on and out to mountains I'd heard of, to this thing, the *sea,* only a word to someone of my land-locked childhood but the dazed, bluest eye of it, multiplied way past eight zillion times.

That something sharp and tangled caught in me: what to call it exactly? We kept going, into day two's long afternoon. Forgive me: I'm cutting ahead to that place for a moment, to us waiting for ride number whatever-it-was, dropped there a good long time by this time, midway through Nebraska. Was it the stillness of old wheat cut down to its jagged quick or that distant line of maple and ash? Was it the darkening sense of all those truly hard crossings and betrayals a century before? Our own waiting—not exactly legendary, its little half-teaspoon of not-quite-misery, three hours now, our hope for the flash of a car, that someone going in the right direction was generous. But it did something, to time.

I see Woody cross-legged on his army tarp—what *did* he carry around inside him from that pointless war?—engrossed in his book, reading right on the shoulder of the road. I walked in circles there, stopping, walked again, empty except for this rush in me. And Frances, distracted, having said nothing to either of us, not even what we were starting to relish from her, a wry comment now and then, some under-the-breath smart-ass remark. Not for a long time. Not since Iowa.

Not until I heard her, behind me.

7

What she said was: pause. What she said was: pause. What she said was: this is no ordinary trip. I think maybe, well, I think you maybe should know that.

Pause.

Because I have to find out.

I knew she meant Ned and the car crash. He was on his way home to her that day. That was the heartthrob part of the story.

No, not really the crash, she said. *Before* the crash. Those months in California, and then in Colorado. I have to go to those places, talk to people.

Well, I said, okay. That's cool.

It's just that, those people know things. And something happened to Ned, I mean *inside*. I have to find out. Shit, this is hard. You know what I mean?

She stood in the wind at an angle somehow, looking both at me and away, bold and fragile, all intertwined.

Sure, I said, I get it.

But I didn't shrug this time, letting the weight of her words sink through me. I didn't want to seem offhand or indifferent. I didn't want to be a nosy jerk about it either. Her life was her life. High up, hundreds of long-winged birds—sandhill cranes, I learned much later—were doing their noisy gaggle en route, headed back north after a warm winter in Mexico or somewhere, clearly into it, clearly honed to their ancient, thrilling task.

8

So this wasn't a blow-it-all-to-hell trip. Jack had been wrong. It was about remembering, finding out. Really the deepest human impulse before that second one: to give up, to let it all go. The plan lay quietly between us; we weren't telling Woody. No point, Frances had said. I had thought—what?—that this was an ordinary trip, spring break famous for such things, our going here, going there, our inch by inch moving west compelling all by itself, our *eyes big as saucers* as we joked in high school. I figured we'd be tourists clicking our cameras though we had none, not even the Brownie Bullet I sent off for in fourth grade, twenty-five cents and the top of some lost cereal box. Gidget goes hitchhiking, Gidget watches the country release whatever it can in the few days we had, all the way west.

The fact is I couldn't believe my good luck. Because it wasn't going to be that. Instead, this would be an honest-to-god *story*. And I'd be in the best position to see it unfold, straight into epic. Because I was merely tagging along, me—the blank slate, the dumb sidekick, the shadow who sees. I'd be invisible. Had I been sucking down novel after novel for nothing? Someone told me once that there were only two narratives in the world: (A) a man goes on a journey and (B) a stranger comes to town. Really the same story, different angles. But we'd be that stranger; this was that journey. Plus we'd be seeing things in that flashing dreamlike way that *getting there fast* always requires. Now there was a weight on all that. Now it weighed ten thousand pounds.

Curiosity can be a knife. It can be sponge. It can fill up the sky with clouds and make you wait there, for something to clear. Because we had a mission. We were *on track*. And Ned. Who was Ned? The world just got huge, as it narrowed.

9

I wonder now about body and soul, the crucial balance between them on such a trip, how it seems at first only little things the body wants grow urgent on the road—where to sleep, what to eat. But you'd be surprised.

More about the Mississippi River guy then, Ed Lutowski, who took us from Rock Island to the western edge of Iowa, to Council Bluffs. He was older, about 60, and a few miles from that mythic river crossing, he did look up, did tell me he'd read *Life on the Mississippi* in high school—in history class, or maybe English. He'd forgotten which.

But I'll tell you, I liked what I read, he said, smiling at me in the rearview mirror.

Mr. Lutowski had been to the cave in Hannibal too, the exact one the actual and original Tom Sawyer and Becky Thatcher got lost in, you know, when those two were still alive. It was something. You guys should go there, he told us. You'd like the place, getting to see what they saw. At this point, Frances jerked awake, grabbed my notebook and scribbled: *What a moron, like fiction is real life*—following her question mark with three big fat exclamation points.

In the front seat, Woody was making an effort: yeah, *Tom Sawyer,* a terrific read, especially that part about the paintbrush. Which is to say, Woody was so much nicer than either Frances or I would ever be. And did I mention that that moron, Mr. Lutowski, let us sleep that first night at his place?

You kids can use my rec room, he said when it got dark in the car. I just finished putting up the knotty pine last week.

His wife, a little standoffish at first, made us supper—*slumgullion,* her name for it, same as my mother's—which turned out to be similar fare: hamburger and tomatoes and onions, all sloshed around in pure grease and piled high on spaghetti—no one called it pasta yet. A scrumptious heart-attack special. There's a lot more where that came from, she told us. Later, we camped on the floor, on these little thick rugs they had, in old sleeping bags their boys left behind.

They're all in the army too, like you were, son, Mr. Lutowski had said to Woody in a sideways way, like it was an important secret between them. Marshall's near Da Nang, last we heard. And Rick's still down at that Mekong Delta in the south. You saw our map in the kitchen. We try to track them best we can. Well. And Scotty—he's the youngest. We don't know where he is, not a thing. He could be anywhere in that country.

Mr. Lutowski looked closely at Woody, in hope, I thought. As if he would know at least one of the boys and have comforting news. Then those two embraced, awkwardly. And it was brief.

Okay, I take it back, Frances whispered to me as Woody conked out first and began quietly to snore. Okay, I'm the moron.

Ride after ride, it was Woody who made sweet contact with the great world, via every driver, *showing interest* as my mother always advised. And in all those conversations, giving every subject a shot whether he knew squat about it or not.

I'm just going with the flow, girls, he'd say, slipping into what he called "hippie talk" when we'd razz him without mercy between rides. And I'm telling you girls—here he'd pause, for a dramatic half-second—this is one big-ass flow.

It was a bit off, that phrasing. But we got the drift. While Frances and I moved in and out of thoughts about Ned, whatever dark lay there, Woody was *on*—today, tomorrow, who knows how long—coming back to life. A free man for the first time in two years, he was having a swell time.

10

The thing about hippies was: we never thought ourselves included in that sweep—no one I knew, at least—a term made up by *Life* magazine probably, or *Newsweek*. It was not a self-anointed demographic in 1971. But the name always seemed hokey, a grand and stupid reduction like most generalizations. The deepest truth is quirky, unaccountably individual. But so many of us looked the part by then, the kneejerk idea of *hippie*. Certainly parents bought into that and worried.

Because it was pretty much standard issue for anyone under 25: dress-down grubby though every detail was carefully, almost religiously, thought out. You're just a reverse snob, that's all, my mother decided, having given up her hope that my college wardrobe would be cured by *Seventeen* magazine. The real dress code: some mix of the seriously worn—just short of worn-out—those blue jeans, turtlenecks, flannel shirts, sandals or work boots, old army jackets or navy pea coats, Indian print bedspreads made into skirts, now and then a peace sign hung or pinned or painted on, those macramé belts that never fastened right, the ubiquitous small, beat-up canvas backpack or shoulder bag. Long hair, of course, on pretty much everyone, and the bra was history, not even quaint. But none of this automatically *meant* anything; it wasn't exactly *I see by my outfit*. It was way more confusing than that, more complex.

Case in point: my friends Nell and Stuart in Champaign, probably the most countercultural sorts you might find, given the look of them, though Stuart had a scary greaser touch too, his old black motorcycle jacket, proof. But everything else, including his toking up half the time, said he was a card-carrying member of that great and growing fringe that would scorn such a card.

Still, it was tricky. I overheard them once, Nell and Stuart back from some wild party at the edge of town, a bonfire there and live music, no doubt a local band droning on, making its screeching stabs in the dark and, I figured, a ton of weed and hash and beer to be had as the night flickered on. They'd come back to Della Crooks' boarding house where Nell and I were roommates, walking in flushed and giggling and no doubt stoned out of their minds. There were so many *hippies* there, I heard Nell say with amusement and half-horror as if she and Stuart had only gone to witness, to be wry and apart, to report later like the most alert anthropologist, which was, in fact, what Nell was studying to be. Oh Stuart, all those *hippies,* Nell the ultimate hippie—by my faulty lights—said again, laughing.

What was that line of an old Louis MacNeice poem? I think now—something about *oh world, so incorrigibly plural.* Or that nugget out of the great blurry dictums my mother loved to intone, this one starting out as simple advice for finding lost keys before it morphed itself vast. *Look under something,* she kept reminding me.

11

What's the deal here, man? said Woody, walking over to us as we hit hour number four of our long wait-for-a-ride. Good job, Nebraska! he called out, his whole body going rigid as he saluted wheat field upon wheat field, the longest horizon going.

Not one damn car, Frances said. I don't get it. Where is everyone? Anyway, I have to pee, she said, eyeing a particularly tall clump of bushes we'd scouted out earlier.

Maybe it's the end of the world, I said, trying to sound upbeat. Maybe everyone else has been incinerated or they're down in their bomb shelters, fighting over the canned peas.

That was one way to pass the time, those nuclear war visions of our childhood, the H-bomb drills in school as routine as the ones we did every few weeks for fire, only instead of fleeing the building, one after another to line up neatly on the playground, we'd hug our knees under our desks and pray madly for the conversion of Russia. I'd gone to Catholic school where it was all magical thinking.

Woody shrugged. Looks like a storm, he said.

That seemed right. Clouds to the west had that eerie snow-darkness about them; the wind was up. Weather moves east, Woody added in the most ominous jokey way, forcing his eyebrows up then down.

It occurred to me: this was just the moment for St. Anthony. I fished around in my pack for my folded-up holy card. He looked a little non-productive, kind of a deadbeat in the picture, holding a leafy sort of thing, staring off in the distance. Not like St. Christopher on *his* holy card who had a mission and a burden and was grimly trudging through water up to his hips. I began to tell Woody and Frances about St. Anthony, my voice rising, a weird liturgical cheerleader waving a pompom. Actually, I added at the end, Tony's the only thing from Catholicism that *does* work. That said, I was half expecting lightning to hit.

I don't get it, Woody said. We say this prayer, this jingle, what for?

It's just like I said. St. Anthony's the patron saint of lost things. He finds stuff. I mean it. But you have to keep looking hard for those things as you say the prayer. Otherwise, all bets are off.

You Catholics! said Frances, throwing her head back. Jesus.

Lapsed Catholic, I said. That *lapsed* part was a point of pride with me.

Yeah, said Woody, but *look hard for stuff*—where? I mean, we can't just *look* for a ride like a glove or a watch that might turn up in a lost and found box. Come on. You know what? This is dumb. And Woody buttoned the top of his army jacket.

But I did, I got them to say that prayer, out in that wide Nebraska sweep as we turned toward the ramp to stare a rescuing car out of pure air:

Dear St. Anthony, please look around.
Something is lost that must be found.

It would be great to say: just then a car drove up. I'd like to claim that. But it took a while. Slow day on the prairie, St. Anthony or not. Or at least on this ramp outside of McCool Junction where we had had such hope, given that name. I mean, how cool is McCool? Frances practically sang when we were dropped there. But four hours now, apparently beyond cool, downright freezing.

Another forty minutes passed. Small flakes started to come down, the sky, though early afternoon, as moody as twilight. Woody reported that almost all the food the Lutowskis had given us in Council Bluffs—peanut butter sandwiches, apples, a few Oreos: zip, long gone. We'd eaten everything way *before* lunch.

Don't worry, I kept telling them, Tony's the man. We most definitely were in the queue. But maybe a lot of people were on his case right now, to find things. The world was a mess, after all. So I blathered on.

Suddenly—how could it feel so sudden when we'd waited that long?—we spotted a car, no, a VW van turning down the ramp, coming toward us. Two freaky types were in there, two scrawny-looking guys, with scraggly beards.

Looks like a real live hippie van to me, Frances said. Look, they're slowing up!

They were. They were pulling over.

12

It was one knockout van, that's sure. Your classic case, or trying hard to be: spray-painted in DayGlo colors, bad R. Crumb rip-offs, cartoon guys angled as far back as they could and still be upright, walking all over the side and up onto the roof in those big shoes and, scattered about, old familiars even then, cast in tall capital letters: KEEP ON TRUCKIN' and ALL YOU NEED IS LOVE, that sort of thing. GIVE PEACE A CHANCE and FLOWER POWER and TUNE IN, DROP OUT.

Woody eased into a faint whistle. Shit, you've got to be kidding.

Hey, this is the Midwest, Frances said. We have to work over-time. We're just now catching up to the coast. Besides, they look young. They're babies.

Bingo!—I guess, Woody said.

Yeah, well. . . . Who cares? I said. Listen, St. Anthony came through! I wanted to savor this; I wasn't going to trade down this moment of Tony triumph for any cultural critique.

Maybe we *were* hallucinating.

No, because I heard the van shifting down, coughing, yanked up to stop. And yes, the door opened out—not a slider, that came later. This was the old regular sort of VW door.

You guys! the driver shouted. You headed somewhere?

A quick decision: tell all, or part? West! Frances yelled, going for general. Then: Denver! Or—she stopped here, weighing the situation. California! she said at last.

All right! Cal-i-for-ni-a! Far out, far fucking out! cried the other guy in pure jubilance, the one in tie-dye everything: T-shirt and jacket and headband awhirl in blues and reds, what we could see from the road anyway.

The driver turned to him: slap me five, bro! Then faced us again. Yo! California! Get your asses in here! We got everything you want in this here friggin' remarkable van!

13

Now *where* in California? the tie-dye guy riding shotgun said to us once Woody and I wedged ourselves in the second seat, and Frances slipped further back, behind us. He had turned around and I could see he was a bit younger than we were, but not by much. He put on his wire-rims so he could check us out.

Wow, you in the army, man? he asked Woody, who had taken off his stocking cap. It's that hair. It gave him away.

Yep. Well, no—just out, in fact. That's it for me and Uncle Sam, forever and ever. I'm out of there.

He was a medic, I jumped in. He's really a CO.

A CO? the driver yelled out, over the racket of the van. Right on! But I thought that meant you didn't have to do nothing except maybe work in a nursing home or teach in the ghetto or something, stateside.

Not according to my draft board, Woody shouted back. I thought that too. No such luck.

Bummer, man. I mean, I hear you, Tie-Dye said. And yeah, I heard that, you know. About how every draft board is different. Then he looked intrigued. Hey, how was it over there, man? Lots of good dope, right? *Pow pow pow pow!* He spun out his forefinger, firing his hand in a wide half-circle. I bet you saw plenty of blood and guts too.

Woody turned away, staring out the window. I could see he really didn't want this conversation to go on. But I could also see those guys would be fine with that. They weren't going to call him a baby killer or ask him about our policy with Red China or what he thought the ethics were, our using Agent Orange. These guys weren't brainiacs, by a long shot. They just wanted to fill the air with noise and beyond that, have a good time. But Woody shut down.

Hey, well. Let's celebrate you getting your CO ass out of there, man, shouted the driver in a magnanimous sort of way. Let's break out the tow-truck reefer!

He means, said Tie-Dye, the really *good* stuff. Like: *call the tow truck, I am wrecked!*

The driver turned on the music, Crosby, Stills and Nash. Blaring. And then the strobe light they had somehow wired up to the overhead fixture.

Cool, huh? Got that on sale, at the only Head shop they got in the dumbshit place we come from. By the way, he shouted back, you guys been to Woodstock?

Nope, not me, I said, not these two either. I actually was guessing that but neither Frances nor Woody stirred up to contradict me.

Too bad, he said. Cuz we're collecting Woodstock stories so we can say we did that stuff, you know? Like we'd been there. Got all naked and muddy, saw Janis scream her guts out and Jimi do a fucking ab-so-lute *Star-Spangled Banner*!

Before either of 'em croaked last fall, my friend here means, said Tie-Dye, turning around to us. Hey, you guys think he set fire to his guitar at Woodstock too? Hendrix, I mean. That would have been ultra out-stand-ing. I bet he did. And he played with his teeth sometimes. I heard that before too. How many guitars you think he fried like that?

Woo-ee! the driver sang out. Wish we coulda went!

Frances shifted back into the beanbag chair they'd set up as the third seat behind Woody and me, those guys at it for a while, remembering in great detail a long list of outrageous things they never witnessed. I closed my eyes, leaned against the window, and wondered if Frances was thinking about Ned or the how long this ride would be or maybe nothing at all.

And Tie-Dye started rolling joints.

14

That's pretty much what it was like when you got picked up by anyone under 30. They brought out the weed and turned up the music; they passed around what food they had; they drove all night, taking turns at the wheel while you slept as best you could, propped up against your backpack. That van though—it seemed a particular miracle that no cop stopped us. You'd think that homemade R. Crumb paint job would be a major tip-off to the world-o-reefer inside. It was practically a theme park in there. But nothing ever happened. No interest. It's like we drove on in a bubble.

Tie-Dye and his friend were from Lincoln, the pinnacle, they said, the *polis* of Nebraska. *Fucking polis* were their exact words. *Of the great state of Nebraska*! They loved to say that, over and over. That *great* in there really cracked them up. That's the only reason they'd watch political conventions on TV, they said. All those stiffs with megaphones prefacing their vote count with *the great state* of whatever—Maine or Texas or Florida or Illinois. No matter. *Mr. Chairman, the great state of Rhode Island proudly casts its pathetic, infinitesimally small and perfectly worthless number of votes for that total loser: Harvey W. Poindexter the third!!* At times it became *Harvey Buttface*—that *Buttface* in quotes they'd dramatically make in the air—*W. Poindexter the*

Third, and occasionally they did a version with *Harve,* in the same exaggerated air-written quotes. Whatever way, it always killed them. They'd laugh like maniacs, taking turns intoning that, stoned or not. What *primo* bullshit! Tie-Dye liked to say. Then it was primo everything for a while: the primo joint he just rolled, the primo map of the western states on the dashboard, the primo box of Cheerios crushed under the seat.

Those guys were definitely not political; they lived in the upper stratosphere where they'd gotten out of the draft. We couldn't figure how since they didn't appear to be in school, with a deferment coming that way. But they were headed to Sacramento, where Tie-Dye had a cousin. They figured they'd like the girls there. Or the girls would like them, better than in Lincoln. That got them too, laughing until they nearly choked. Oh yeah, they'd say to each other, oh yeah! Those girls will like us *way* better. I really didn't want to know what that meant.

Maybe their IQs are too low, even for the army, Frances said to us at a rest stop while they were in the can.

Too low for the army? Woody said. Not possible.

The other thing about getting picked up by people our age was the stoned toys they'd bring out. *That* cracked us up. After a few rounds, passing the joint, sure enough those toys would appear, treasures to be shared. Pointless, beautiful toys like thick blue waves trapped in a see-through plastic box. You'd sit there and hold it with both hands, lifting one side a little, then the other. And the waves would do their thing and make an ocean. It definitely helped to be stoned. Those Lincoln boys had an array of such items. The driver's first promise was true: theirs was one friggin' remarkable van. And that old VW cut through the mountains all right.

Mountains! Do you believe it? That all this piled up rock could *look* this way? Tie-Dye said in a hushed tone way past Cheyenne, almost to Laramie. A moment of genuine poetry. So we stopped the van, staring out and up.

Hey, check out that sign: *Scenic Overlook,* Tie-Dye would say then as we passed through what was left of Wyoming, into Utah and Nevada. He'd open his arms wide. That's a goddamn command, he'd tell us repeatedly. It's required, man. It's the law. Hey, they'll arrest us right here, no shit, right this second unless we sit back on our thumbs for a while to just gaze!

15

It wasn't all sleep and stare, stop and be hypnotized by beauty. We invented various games to pass the time in that van, like *First Memory* or *Famous Last Words*. Or our favorite: *Moment of History*.

Ok, said Woody, clue #1: there's a guy in a hat.

We all went blank.

And a second guy, he said, walking away, out of the TV screen, in handcuffs.

We shrugged.

Come on, guys, think hard!

You come on, said Frances, these clues bite.

Out the window, beyond the genuine postcard-of-the-west mountains, close up or snow-rimmed in the distance, we'd seen canyons and salt flats and high desert. Day into night into day again, we'd been driving that long.

Okay, okay, Woody said, so the guy in the hat is older, the handcuffed guy younger. The older guy is rushing into the frame, from the right. Woody looked at us expectantly like he was willing the gears in our heads to turn. But they were locked; they needed more oil.

All right. Here's the clincher. The guy in the hat has a gun. He's waving it. He's shooting it, and the crowd around them—they're inside some public building—is totally freaking out.

Teacher teacher teacher, call on me! Please please please! shouted Tie-Dye's friend who was driving again. I know! I know! Jack Ruby, right? And he's offing Lee Harvey Oswald right on TV—I saw that, man! With my own personal eyeballs!

Bingo, brother, said Woody, glancing at Frances and me with pity, like: *really, you guys are pathetic. That was yours!* And then he pointed low toward the front seat and shook his head. But next, it was the driver's turn since he had guessed right.

Okay, he began, there's these caves, see, and we're underground. And there's this really creepy music. Got it?

What you talking, boy? said Tie-Dye. What caves? You wasted or something?

No! Just caves, man, all wet-like and gummy, and this music, like: woo oo oo oo, woo oo oo oo. You know.

We need better clues than that, Woody said. And are you sure this is history?

Yes, ab-so-lute-ly, said the driver. So these creatures, man-like guys but not really human, start coming right out of the walls. Really creepy, like I said. One arm, then one leg, a whole bunch of them until they're walking around all crooked, stick-like, in the cave. And making these little mumbling sounds and shit, because their mouths don't work too good.

Oh, I know I know, screamed Tie-Dye. It's those clay people, right? From that old *Flash Gordon* episode. I'm right, right?

Yeah oh yeah! his friend shouted, hitting the steering wheel, honking the horn.

There was no telling those guys what *was* history and what *wasn't*. I remembered that scene too, on channel five, the old Buster Crabbe version of *Flash Gordon* run late every Sunday morning in Chicago when I was little. My brother and I would rush home from Mass to watch it. I loved those clay people. We'd often mimic them around the kitchen table, walking stiff-legged to that weird music, doing the mumble and the sing-song and driving our mother insane.

Not history, man, Woody said. Sorry, you're disqualified. That's just TV. Actually, not even TV. They made that series in the '30s or something, and ran it at the movies first.

Maybe not *your* history, Tie-Dye said. Hey, it's a big world out there, man. You got to open your mind!

We carried on, mostly into more genuine historical moments, the recent moon landing, for instance, with that giant dusty bootprint of Neil Armstrong the major clue. And what singer turned up on Ed Sullivan, minus a pelvis?

Elvis! shouted Frances, right off. But that one was easy.

Okay, I said, how about this: a zillion wild, long-haired people screaming against the war in a park.

That could be anywhere, Frances said.

Okay, but floor-to-ceiling plate-glass windows are breaking, and Norman Mailer is there, and someone is wearing a *F-u-c-k* headband. And here's a hint: *Revolution for the Hell of It.* I did the finger-quote thing on that.

Abbie Fucking Hoffman! yelled Tie-Dye. Hey, I saw that book in a store! And that's the convention the Democrats did last time, in Chicago, right? Shit. Wish we would've been there too. Sounds like that was a gas-a-roonie!

I was afraid the thought of any political convention would trigger their *great state of whatever* number again. But it didn't. We all got quiet instead, sunk back to that remarkable spectacle, one we all wished we'd seen for ourselves. I had been 18, a city bus ride away but my mother wouldn't allow me to go. The odd thing was that *she* had gone down to the Loop that week, though not really *there* there. She and a friend had tickets for the old Auditorium Theater one of those convention nights, where Art Linkletter was doing some show. She was really excited about that, seeing him live, on stage, an old hero of hers. I loved the irony of that from the first minute. The world shattering outside, everyone young gone freaking crazy while inside that theater my mother was happily watching Art Linkletter, whose claim to fame when I was a kid was his TV show *House Party* and its memorable segment *Kids Say the Darndest Things.* And there they were, all grown up saying those darndest things out there in the street, on Michigan Avenue near Buckingham Fountain, zany and earnest, setting fire to Chicago and the whole idea we should ever go to war.

Wait, I got one, Tie-Dye's friend said though he could hardly get it out, he was so pumped. Bubble bubble bubble, he said, turning back to us as he drove, his face completely lit up.

What? Bubble bubble bubble? Woody said. Hey, keep your eyes on the road! Anyway, I give up. You're nuts, you know that? You guys don't follow the rules. Jeez.

Oh man, the driver said, looking up in the rearview mirror now, bubble bubble bubble! Come on, man, you remember. That's *Sea Hunt. Mike Nelson,* he slowly intoned, *underwater diver.* Man, that's the en-ti-re fucking soundtrack from TV—bubble bubble bubble! Fuck you!

But my favorite real *Moment of History* started with a microphone, a small crowd, then something high and shaped like a massive capsule you'd swallow whole floating into the frame. The film quality was bad, I told them, all gritty and full of black spots. Then the announcer broke into sobs, half way through: *oh, it's burning, it's burst into flames, ladies and gentlemen, I can't talk, it's . . . masses of smoking wreckage!* I kept handing them more and more clues until I practically gave away the answer.

But no one put it together. Maybe they hadn't been addicted to that old Walter Cronkite show, *The Twentieth Century,* which ran every week, remarkable footage from both World Wars, the jazz era, the Depression. My brother and I had watched that every Sunday night, before supper. But this particular moment—I kept seeing the dirigible again, the Hindenburg, that famous clip of it catching fire in 1937, coming apart, right there in the air. Really, it's the announcer's voice I still hear, transformed in a second from its breezy newsman run-of-the-mill cadence to *oh the smoke and the flames, oh, the humanity!*—mid-air, the most heart-shattering anguish imaginable.

16

The whole time Frances kept insisting: there wasn't any reason to tell Woody about Ned. The plan was, of course, that he'd be breaking off from us, heading north to see his folks in Oregon once we got to California. Anyway, what was there to say? She wanted to listen to anyone who remembered Ned, that's all. To put two and two together. It wasn't like I was her best buddy and she was confiding in me. I'd only get the scoop because I was tagging along and would be meeting those people. And that would happen after Woody split, up the coast. It's not exactly that we knew stuff and he didn't. I didn't know anything yet, only that it was out there somewhere. And maybe it would come.

We stopped a little longer at one of those scenic overlooks, coming into California from Nevada, Tie-Dye and his friend ready for their *spiritual practice*—another phrase they set in high fingered quotes. They sat cross-legged on a blanket about seventy yards from us, their mouths opening and closing in a set rhythm they'd concocted, what they called the *meta-yoga-silent-sing-along* part of their method, the warm-up maybe.

Frances had wandered off somewhere. I saw how Woody watched her disappear into the woods, beyond the restrooms. In some ways, she was nondescript, ordinary—average height, on the thin side—but that silky black hair, and *good bones* you might say now of such a face, but mainly it was something more mysterious that made people look back, look again. The tentative, almost delicate way of bringing her hand to her lip when she thought hard about something, or she could go fierce, turning her head in disdain or in a sudden softening of whatever, a moment ago, she was certain she believed—that surprise, those shifts. Her smart, ironic approach to the world seemed, at certain times, to include you, not cut you out of the secret. She was the kind of person I was glad to travel with, if only because she'd obviously be the magnet, the one everyone, males especially, would glom onto so I could rest easy. On the ramps, our thumbs out: hey, you're the most *visible,* Frances, you should be the one they see first, you know what I mean? That was Woody's low-key way of acknowledging this thing about her.

But like I said, it was agreed Woody would be left out of the whole Ned thing. So when he asked if he could talk to me privately about something, I was fairly sure it didn't concern Frances.

This is about Crazy Alex, isn't it?

Why would I want to talk about Alex?

Come on, Woody.

He looked out over the ridge into the valley way below, past the iron fencing and the sign warning parents to keep their small children far far away from the edge, *under any circumstance.* But to read the sign at all, you had to walk up pretty close—with those very kids screaming and wiggling and hanging on to you, if you had any.

So, he said. So. Do you know *why*?

Why she dumped you?

She really didn't dump me.

Right, Woody. Sure. Get real.

Okay, he said.

Then it came to me: I didn't want to tell him. I tried to backpedal.

Listen Woody. It's none of my beeswax. What do I know about you guys? As a couple, I mean. And you and me, we've been in the same room, how many times? I mean before this trip.

But you *know*, don't you? She talks to you. He picked up a small white stone and threw it, a high loop, over the railing. We lost sight of it in seconds.

Well, maybe I do, I don't know.

I was no good at this, a terrible liar and an even worse truth teller. Now I'd be the bad guy. It wasn't fair. Why hadn't Alex told him herself? She'd be furious with me for saying anything.

Then you have to tell me, he said simply. And looked straight at me.

She has certain ideas, Woody, I said, stalling. You know Alex.

Keep going.

She thinks you're, well. . . .

He hadn't looked away. He was still staring at me, the mountains and valley behind him big and solemn as some wide-screen movie pan.

Oh, screw this. To be drop-dead honest, Woody, she thinks you're dull. That's what she said. I'm sorry. I know you've been together for almost three years now, since that lame-o dance in high school, and you've been back here on leave and everything.

But not talking much. I guess that's the trouble, the not-talking part. That's where she gets this dull business.

I could tell Alex's take wasn't a major shock to him. Dull people usually know they're dull. Like fat people know they're fat. Not stupid people. They never seem to know how stupid they are and keep trying to convince the world otherwise. But I'd noticed that a lot of the dull do it for solace, a way to be private about things, to get on with what they want to think about, quietly, in secret. I felt pretty much like that, most of the time.

Dull doesn't mean not smart, I went on. It just means dull. It's a matter of style, Woody. You aren't a flashy guy, that's all. It's not exactly a death sentence. It's actually something to be proud of. But in fact, I think this trip is bringing out another side of you, don't you? I mean, talking to all these strangers? And getting out of the army?

I paused for a second. Alex should see you now!

I was fast entering the realm of feel-good blather, a lower form of metaphysics. The bullshit factor loomed large. But Woody did seem to be changing; *coming out of his shell* is what we would have called it in my house. He was loosening up. Even Frances had remarked on that.

To tell the truth, this makes me feel pretty crappy, he said.

Look it, Woody, I said. Alex is *Crazy* Alex for a reason. We're talking about someone who cuts off her pubic hair, glues it to the wall and calls it art. I looked away for a second. You know *that* little number of hers, don't you?

Woody half-smiled. Yeah, she took a picture and sent it to me. The guys in my unit thought, well, highly of that, put it that way.

Yeah, well, *dull* next to that is pretty freaking normal, seems to me. We're all dull as dust against that model. You guys are just too different, that's all.

Alex had done that thing with her pubic hair. A lot of weirder stuff too. In our all-girl high school, St. Pat's, at that dance, for instance, the one she dragged Woody to—really our senior prom but the Archbishop of Chicago had forbidden anyone to call it that—she'd brought a vial of mercury, thick quicksilver gotten from five thermometers she broke on purpose just to roll that stuff around on the tables, on those linen tablecloths. Toxic as hell, little shiny beads of it. But beautiful and surreal. Woody must have remembered that. We were always shaking our heads about Alex then, like when she announced she was going down to the bus station in the Loop every Saturday afternoon for one full month to pick up sailors—her duty as a citizen of the world, she said—and take them to the Art Institute. And maybe she did.

Well, okay, said Woody, but you know what bugs me about this? How do I say this? He stopped for a moment, but didn't dare look at me.

Woody, you don't have to explain anything. I swear I. . . .

Yeah, like I'm quiet, I am, he continued. Hey, you try to get a word in edgewise with Alex. You know how it is. She's nonstop. She's all at once. Anything and everything, she's got some theory about it. I love that. Okay, but this not-talking thing, this dull thing? That really gets me.

Woody was on a roll now, warming to his subject. He turned abruptly toward me.

Because you know what?

What?

I was a medic over there, right? You know what that really means? *What a cool job, Woody. Like, so damn noble, you being a CO and all.* Yeah, right. It means I tried to take care of people, that's all. Not that I was that good at it either. Guys with their faces half blown off, their backs broken, hips crushed, their skin burned and blistered. And all for what?

Listen Woody. It was important, brave stuff you did over there. Especially since those pinheads drafted you. You were a CO, for god's sake. By definition, you weren't supposed to go. That was totally illegal, as far as I'm concerned. You gave it your all anyway.

See, that's exactly what I mean.

A big white Buick pulled up and a family poured out: Mom, Dad, a couple of rangy teenagers—two boys—and a medium-sized spotted dog, all excited about the view. We watched them move down the platform. But Woody wasn't finished.

Hear me out, would you? Remember that map of 'Nam back in Mr. Lutowski's kitchen? I have to tell you: I could hardly look at that thing. It makes me sick. This fucking war. Some of those guys so bad off, Torpedo begging me to just do him in, please, right now. And you know what? It would have been a lot fucking kinder to do that. Lugger who dropped acid, tripping his brains out, or like Warhorse and Spinner just stoned out of their minds, paranoid, spooked by anything that moved. Imagine a guy like that with a M16 in his hands, aiming it god-knows-where. And I'm going to talk about that? With Alex, who knows everything about everything already? Or at parties? Right. Everyone all into peace and love and head-in-the-sand, hey, wow, let's just be mellow, man. I mean, look at those guys: perfect example.

Woody pointed to Tie-Dye and his friend, who were onto their version of the *om* thing, trying their best to be serious between bouts of snorting, wheezing laughter.

Do you actually think, Woody went on, that those two want to know the shit I saw over there? Or anyone? You kidding me? That's why I love this stupid babbling I can do in cars, with whatever driver, all these strangers. I can hide in it. TV shows, basketball, the best hamburger joint, you name it, just pure bullshit. Easy stuff to talk about. Practically a way *not* to talk. I'm like some photographer, you know, who never has to be in the picture.

We just stood there at that point, looking out at what had been officially announced *scenic* by someone in an office. Not that that mattered to the valley, as if it needed a caption. Those mountains still opened up, all the colors that stone and earth can be—the lush brown and pine green, distant snow edging the higher places, immense shadows shifting below us because way above, the clouds kept moving.

Well, I can see how that would make anyone clam up, I said.

It was true. It shut me down too, just hearing that much. He'd been at the heart of it. Horrible stuff. I didn't know what to say. And then I was saying it.

Except, look Woody. I stared hard at him. Screw Alex. I mean, I've known her forever. She's great, in her way. But you're better off without her.

Woody was already embarrassed about his outburst, it was clear. He was avoiding my eye again, finding more small stones, turning over every one in his hand like each was utterly fascinating, a perfect little world unto itself. That took a while.

Yeah, he said finally. Yeah, and you're right probably. Your point before, that thing about Alex and me being awful different. I guess I sort of knew that.

We got quiet all over again. Woody's default mode was, after all, to agree, be silent and polite, more sad than pissed off. He had a handful of stones now. Stepping forward, he threw the whole lot of them over the ridge. They sprayed out in all directions.

What will you do in Oregon, Woody? You going to stay up there?

I don't know. My dad thinks I should work at his grocery store for a while, and then apply to U of O or Portland State. I have the GI bill, you know. It's a pretty good deal.

You could study medicine. All that experience in the field.

I never want to think about that again, he said.

17

We were almost to Sacramento where Woody would be taking off alone, up Route 5, straight into Oregon. We'd lose Tie-Dye and his friend too. They were busy trying to remember where the cousin lived, what street exactly and where on that street, the guy Tie-Dye said would be out of his gourd with joy and amazement to see them. *Total and complete, no-doubt-about-it ecstasy* is how he put it as his friend nodded happily.

Outside it was semi-*other*. Ordinary orchards, of course, but we spotted palm trees and signs for almond groves. Vineyards too, with grapes and grapes and more grapes, distant rows and rows of twisted tied-up branches, vast fiefdoms for table wine. There must have been oranges and lemons lurking somewhere too, but probably further south where it got even sunnier. And farther than that—if you could believe the postcards on racks at gas stations—farmers grew the wildest things imaginable on trees—avocadoes, which I had never eaten in my life. I'd never even *seen* one.

The truth is I was astounded that we'd gotten all that way so fast. It was only Monday. It took those pioneers over a year to cross what we just cut though in three days: mountains you couldn't count, and rivers and prairies. And those were the

speedy ones, without grandma in tow, with extra wheels for their
wagon stashed in the back, next to the cornmeal.

Well, this is it, said Woody as we neared the junction of 80 and
5, and pulled over into the broken asphalt parking lot of some
root beer joint.

Hey, no fair, man! Tie-Dye said. Where's the girls on roller
skates? The ones to bring us our root root root beer? Not one
appeared. It was a low-budget sort of place.

That's *southern* California, Dimbo, his friend said, that's where
the girly roller skaters hang out.

We had stuffed our winter coats and gloves and hats into our
backpacks. We were in T-shirts now. Very weird, for March. It
was warm, standing in the sun on that asphalt.

Listen Woody, I said, keep in touch, will you? I want to know
what you're doing, school or whatever else. It was great having
you along. I mean it.

Me too, said Frances.

I was surprised at how hollow I felt, and scared suddenly. And
how stupid and predictable and unconvincing those good-bye
words sounded however much I tried to intensify the *I mean it*
part, to code it with affection. Then I was angry and sad. We had
a nice drill going, the three of us. A sweet balance of earnest and
funny, urgent and indifferent, silence and talk. I liked the guy a
lot. He was good through and through. And our conversation
on the overlook in Nevada, his stone after stone picked up so
carefully then flung out over the ridge. *Look under something.* I

thought briefly about Alex—an idiot. My friend, of course. But still an idiot.

Yeah, I will. I'll let you know about stuff, Woody said, and thanks. He had written down our addresses in the van. He looked like he was going to cry. Well, gotta go, he said, hugging us both surprisingly hard, turning quickly away to walk up the street.

I bet he doesn't look back, said Frances.

18

That's one cool man-o-man, Tie-Dye's friend said back in the van.

Yeah, said Tie-Dye, turning to Frances and me. Why doesn't one of you two, you know, jump his sorry bones? What's with you girls? I don't get you.

Pretty soon we'd be leaving the van too. They took us only a little ways, where the old Sacramento Historical Park cut into 80. They were headed north, they said, then maybe a little east, still not clear where the cousin lived in town. That piece of paper with the crucial information, they assumed it was in the glove compartment. But it had vanished.

Poof! said Tie-Dye. But Confucius say: Nothing worthwhile easy gotten, no no! And both started their manic laughter again.

Thanks a million, Frances said, grabbing her backpack. You guys took us a hell of a long way.

Yeah, I said. We're grateful.

No prob-lem-o, they said, nearly in unison.

You three made this one *primo* trip, said Tie-Dye's friend.

With that, the primo thing started up again: the primo weather out here, what primo you-know-whats on those girls walking by, how primo the cars were in California, their having counted five primo convertibles so far, of various primo colors, how primo hungry they were, speaking of lunch.

No one had spoken of lunch, but Frances and I were stepping down, out of the van. We were waving. They were laying on the horn then, making the peace sign at us, tearing off in a sudden right-hand turn.

19

California. Here we were. Frances smiled a little wanly, and not at me. At the thought of it, I guess. At all that lay ahead.

See, she said, I told you, you do need sunglasses here. That got me fishing the cheapo pair out of my pack, and I put them on. Sunglasses in March. Like some movie star.

We didn't wait long. Another hippie van pulled over, this one not so freshly or enthusiastically christened as such, with its blistering blue paint, its one cracked window repaired with duct tape. The genuine article, I suppose you might say, clearly on the road for a while. We heard a voice: *just get in the back!* So we opened the rear double door and heaved up, into the thing, settling down, looking toward the driver's seat, past all the predictables: the sway of hanging beads on the windows, pillows and Indian print spreads piled high, *Zap Comix* and *Rolling Stone* magazines lying about, *The Whole Earth Catalog* on top of everything, its black cover floating our home planet seen far away, from outer space. We could make out the two in the front seat, their long hair, their T-shirts, thin leather strips around their necks, one in a Mao cap—the usual get-up, all of which spelled *cool,* spelled *young.* Then they turned around. News flash: they were old, nearly as old as my parents, I remember thinking. Some of their teeth were missing. They looked awful.

Frances elbowed me fast and hard. We were careful not even to glance at each other. I flashed on a new, abrupt fact: this has been going on for years and years out here. These were probably old beats, *beatniks* turned *into* hippies, right? This was history, an honest tradition by now in California. And I remembered another shock, a fact I discovered earlier that year: Allen Ginsberg was only five years younger than my mother. He could have been her little brother. Unlike the Midwest where all this seemed fresh and alive, out here it had been eons, and much darker stuff. That meant Altamont and the Manson trial, and Timothy Leary busted for drugs, all—admittedly—a vague jumble in my head. I didn't read the newspapers and had no TV. I felt it though, a dramatic shift in climate.

Still, the woman turned to us the way a well-meaning aunt might have at the Thanksgiving table, polite, almost interested. Where you from? she asked.

Illinois, Frances said.

The woman looked uncertain. She might have been tuning in that puzzle we did as kids, trying to find the piece labeled *Illinois* to pop into place somewhere in the middle of that busy map. I'd always been proud that my state was shaped weirdly, like a lucky rabbit's foot, I thought, calling just enough attention to itself and no more.

The Midwest, Frances self-corrected. Not too far from Chicago.

Oh, Chicago, the woman said. I know that place.

You absolutely know that place, the man driving said, a great meaning in his voice.

I couldn't tell if that was good meaning or bad, or something in between. Better not to ask. Besides, their being older made us shy.

Where you going? the man called back to us.

San Francisco, Frances told him.

We can take you as far as Berkeley, he shouted over the outside traffic. Or a little farther, to Oakland maybe, though it's past where we're going. I could drop you near the bridge there. Is that okay?

Far out, she shouted back.

Well, dears, the woman said, half-facing us again and giving a little wave, welcome to California!

20

We couldn't see much through the windows of that van, with those beads shifting back and forth as we sped west that afternoon, then south on route 80, through Davis and Vacaville, near Napa, past Vallejo. We saw signs for those cities at least, their flashes of green and bright sunlight. Then we were approaching, no, actually entering—clearly a detour, off 80—that most fabled place of all: Berkeley, epicenter of all things freaky and amazing and with-it. I pushed back the strands of beads and held them at an angle to get a longer look. Of course, it was exactly what I thought because clichés are at least partly true: coffee shops galore there, bookstores, all manner of crazies in costume doing street theater, earnest-looking guys right on the sidewalk playing flute as young women, barefoot, in long dresses swayed, stood still, and swayed again. Everyone seemed to be outside, busy with things, at least a fourth of them illegal. Imagine some very hip Richard Scarry cover, set back to 1971, your usual postman and meter maid and kids on their bikes racing next to countless mom-sedans all traded up for this. Inside the van, our driver and his friend appeared oblivious, having slipped into their own universe, shoving into the tape deck the Stones' first album, seemingly on endless return. It kept blaring away, that voice as usual, getting no satisfaction.

I can't believe it, I said quietly to Frances, *Berkeley.* We're in freaking Berkeley, California!

The whole afternoon was in italics. We drove up University Avenue, toward Shattuck.

You two mind if we stop for a second? the driver called out. We have to pick up something.

That's cool, I yelled. Was he kidding?

We pulled over in front of a fire hydrant. If this were Chicago and my father driving, he would have leapt out, grabbed the tall bushel basket from the trunk, dropping it neatly over the hydrant and gone about his business, thinking he'd avoid a ticket that way. But these two could care less, parking so illegally, dashing into a shop with clothes, books, rolling papers in all colors, a mishmash of things on display. A big yellow cat lay in the store window too, staring out at us. A sphinx-cat, its front legs out, perfectly motionless. It could hardly keep its eyes open. Frances and I looked at each other. We climbed out of the van too and stood leaning against it.

A young man was sitting alone on a wooden box over to our right, before a café of some sort. He started to sing, holding his guitar, hitting the strings now and then not like he was interested exactly, more like he had forgotten something then almost remembered. He was dazed, his face wonderfully—what?—vacant, full of nothing. Rich with that nothing.

I should, he half sang, half spoke. And stopped. . . . *have known better . . . a girl like you. . . .* Here he slowed, paused again. *That I would love. . . .* It was quiet again. *Love,* he started and stopped, *love everything that you*—each word damped down now, languid, something secret and marvelous between each one—*that you do . . . and I do, hey hey*—

It wasn't song anymore, not even dream. Nowhere we could follow.

21

Their errand took just a couple of minutes. They carried a couple of small sacks into the van and did a big fat u-turn, right on University Avenue and we were out of there, headed back to route 80. We were approaching the bridge from Oakland to San Francisco, past where our driver had promised to go out of his way to drop us. I pointed this out to Frances, who half-shrugged. Soon he was paying a toll and before long, we were back on land, headed up Market Street.

So where is it exactly you want to go? the driver shouted back to us.

We're in Frisco, right? I said. Gee, thanks a lot. I know this is more than you bargained for. He kept driving. I felt guilty.

That's okay, it all comes back. I swear it does. You two ever heard of Ram Dass?

Actually, I had. Later I'd learn more, about his dad, for instance, his thinking that the stupidest name on earth, especially since his son had a perfectly decent name already—Richard Alpert—so he decided to call him Rum Dum.

Man, Ram Dass is totally in the groove, he continued. That cat knows every inch of the inner realm, how these things add up. Good makes good. He's totally on the bus, you know what I mean? Our driver said that again, only slower, enunciating the phrase: *on the bus.* Not the fractured, delicate way that young man sang his Beatles song. Here each word came down emphatic, a bull's eye, like he was nailing a sign to a wall.

But you know how you said *Frisco* before? Here's a tip: never, never say *Frisco.* Man, that's like something out of Perry Como. Like a thing sleazy Frank might sing about. Well, he actually did sing that. You *do* know I mean Sinatra, don't you?

Or *San Fran,* the woman added. That's not cool either. She said it—*San Fran*—like she was picking up each word with a tweezers.

What was left to call it? But I didn't ask.

Thanks for the info, I said, hoping *info* was an okay abbreviation. But really, I blurted out—then had to raise my voice over a sudden honking war outside, two or three cars' worth—really, this is really really nice of you.

And that address you two girls want? he said.

Um, over near where Steiner crosses Broadway, I think, Frances told him after digging in her pack for a notebook with its addresses and phone numbers. Let's see. Yeah.

Whoa, classy digs! the woman said. Pacific Heights? You *related* to those folks?

I figured she was rethinking their efforts to deliver us, their good will, their taking care of the bridge toll. Maybe this stocking-up-karma thing meant that helping the un-needy wouldn't wash for points.

Old high school friends of my husband's, Frances was saying. But no, I don't know them that well. I haven't seen them in, like, ages.

Husband, is it? The woman turned abruptly to look at us again. At how young we were, I suppose. Clearly a double-take.

So now it's a *husband* we're talking about. Really? You sure about that, sweetie? You *sure* you have a husband?

Sorry, Frances said. I mean, my dead husband.

22

I thought that fairly heartless, playing the dead husband card like that even though the woman was on the obnoxious side. But I didn't say anything. We were standing on Steiner then, trying to scope out where these two lived, these old friends of Ned—Kevin and Joyce Sunderland. But I kept seeing her in my head, that woman rearing back like someone had struck her hard. Then she'd gone quiet. Someone *had* hammered her: Frances. When they dropped us off, I couldn't quite read their faces: were they sad or angry? Embarrassed? I tried to be as grateful as I could, with more slobbering out the usual: really great of you, this helped us a lot, hope you have a nice evening, that stuff. Frances, for her part, said nothing more.

The building was Victorian. Beautiful. Well-kept. It *was* classy. That woman was right. It contained a handful of apartments, a regular mansion turned into those smaller spaces maybe thirty years earlier. Or I'm hallucinating again. No matter. It looked like a grand place to be, especially after those days on the road, cramped and curled up in a van, washing up at rest stops, eating crackers and apples and Hershey Kisses, lulled or blasted to bits by the Doors, the Beatles down their *Abbey Road,* the Jefferson Airplane, Led Zeppelin, and those Lincoln boys' favorite, an old song whose title was buried in the refrain they loved to scream along in unison, banging on the dash and the steering wheel their favorite part:

And you tell me
Over and over and over again my friend
Ah, you don't believe we're
On the eve of de-struc-tion. . . .

So Ned knew the Sunderlands in high school? I said to Frances.

Yeah. Well, you know Ned was older than me. By nearly four years. He dropped out of college, but Kevin, sort of a whiz kid really. They were pals since third grade or something. Joyce too. She was in that same class in DeKalb, so she knew Ned pretty well. In grade school and high school. Kevin went through college in, like, three years, then law school. In Chicago, I think. And now he's got this super hot-shot job out here. Doing what, who the hell knows?

Hence these digs, I said.

Don't worry. They're expecting us. I called them.

How long will we be here?

Not long. Oh yeah, they're putting us up too, Frances said. I figure at least they'll feed us good.

23

Joyce Sunderland was what we called *straight* in those days, before sexual preference had anything to do with it. It meant she wasn't a freak, wasn't even close to a hippie, that she was what her parents had dreamed she would be: well-groomed unto squeaky clean and *upwardly mobile*—a phrase of both description and derision then. Which, in turn, meant she probably hadn't smoked much dope, if any; had gone through school without weeks or months or years taken off to find herself; hadn't wandered, hadn't done time in a coop or a commune. It meant she had a decent job and her stockings no doubt matched her blouse; that she probably hadn't read *Zen Buddhism* by D. T. Suzuki or Kerouac's *On the Road* or *The Magic Mountain* by Thomas Mann or A. S. Neill's *Summerhill* or anything Gary Snyder had written, or Thoreau and Whitman, Scott and Helen Nearing, Hermann Hesse. And countless others, books we read with a thirst having not a whit to do with school, passing them on to friends who took everything the same way, with near religious zeal. Or maybe she did; maybe I'm not being fair.

But she probably never stayed up half the night arguing ideas found on those pages, and no, I'm almost positive she never sat in or held a picket sign to rage against the war or for civil rights. I don't imagine you could superimpose her on that crowd of kids after Kent State either, that moment in time when the riots spread everywhere. Three years later, after college when I worked as a graduate school admissions clerk at Northwestern University doggedly going over transcripts, recalculating each GPA, I'd get to spring 1970 where regular grading suddenly morphed—one term only—to a pass/fail option, school after school, big or small, the madness that universal. Back in Illinois that May, I remember the frats in their Hawaiian shirts who thought it would be a lark to watch the National Guard roll down the street in their jeeps, how even they were instantly politicized. Those business majors, all pepper-sprayed now and enraged, kept using the campus phones in the Student Union to call home. I'd overhear the same half conversation again and again: *No mom, there's no communists here! We weren't doing anything, I swear to God. It's the police. It's the goddamn National Guard—they've gone berserk!* Not that I'd be making such a call to my own mother who had checked out of hearing about drugs, sex, rock and roll—or politics—most emphatically, and probably wisely, the minute my college years began.

But Joyce—the fact remained that she wasn't the sort of person who would be shouting *kill the pigs!* any time soon no matter how much craziness erupted. She had *sold out*—that would be the standard take on her. But in Joyce's case, I'm not sure there ever was any yearning-to-be-free little heart in there to *be* sold. She seemed, quite gladly, to have accepted her straight-arrow fate from the start. Had happily entered what some people called *the American Death Trap.* But the good news for us, it occurred to me then, was that in that trap she might have turned into one fabulous cook, as Frances had halfway implied. I was starving.

She was home when we rang the bell in the vestibule. We heard her cheery voice through the static of the old intercom, a little grill next to their names. I'll buzz you in! she said. We're on the second floor, the right-hand door.

Even the stairway, the public part of that building, was beautiful, pinned down by a thick oriental rug worked up lushly in intricate reds and blacks and light browns. But the Sunderlands' flat—polished wood floors, heavy comfortable couches, oddly delicate overstuffed chairs, more oriental carpets, even in the kitchen. Money *and* taste. A rare combination, it turns out. But this was the first I ever saw such things almost brought together. Their books were the only apparent kink in all this. They had lined up everything perfectly on a single tall set of shelves. Alphabetically, I realized. And nothing looked read, all the spines in perfect shape.

Joyce ushered us in with much graciousness and installed us immediately in the back bedroom with its twin beds under their powder blue spreads—the guest room, she said with pride. She urged us to relax, take a shower, take a nap. Kevin would be home in about an hour. Kevin had a weighty deal pending, with Ajax. So perhaps we'd be celebrating tonight, she said in a particularly sparkly way, doing a quick whirling gesture with her hands, the sort common on TV. And of course there was so much to say about Ned. Here she looked thoughtfully at Frances and the moment slowed to a stop.

Then I was saying *great! thanks!* as Frances disappeared into the bathroom and Joyce slipped out of the room. That seemed to be my major function on the trip right now. I was always saying thanks.

24

Get the hell in here! Frances hoarse-whispered.

I was sitting on the bed, having unearthed most everything in my pack. I was picking through my underwear and shirts, wondering which ones to wash out in the sink.

What? I was walking through the bathroom door. Then: O my god!

Frances was pointing, but she didn't need to. Ned—looking gorgeous and dazed, hair out and out flying, as usual, in all directions—was huge, and laminated somehow, stuck to the wall, the very center of what seemed like a million other pictures in mad rotation around him: Pete Seeger, Twiggy, Robert Kennedy, Woody Guthrie, Winston Churchill, that girl at Kent State, kneeling speechless with her mouth wide open. There was Gandhi, a young John Glenn stepping out of his space capsule, and below him, Buzz Aldrin on the moon with the flag held straight out by a wooden rod sewn into its upper edge to make it fly right in that airless, breezeless atmosphere. Dorothy Day and Bob Dylan were next, then Jane Addams in the doorway of Hull House, and definitely Gene McCarthy, the Beatles, sweet-faced and waving from *The Ed Sullivan Show,* Martin Luther King still standing in Memphis, Robert Frost at Kennedy's inauguration. And so on. And on. All of it overlapped, so where Gandhi's cheek gave way, say, Twiggy's ear began, below her startling short hair. If you used the toilet, you'd be staring right into this spectacle. In fact, you'd be looking straight into Ned's eyes, which someone had pencil-colored green. The rest was in black and white.

A tribute maybe? I said after a moment. Think of it that way, Frances. I mean, look at the company he's keeping—Martin Luther King, Pete Seeger, Robert friggin' Frost, no less.

It was picture after picture, a wildly crowded wheel of time and energy, be it dark or full of light. I stood there, transfixed by all of it, adrift, overwhelmed.

But Frances hadn't taken her eyes off Ned's eyes for a second.

They were blue, light blue, she was saying. Blue, like some really quiet place in the ocean. And fuck them, they *knew* Ned. How could they get that part wrong?

25

I keep thinking about that collage, which was, in fact, a rather popular thing to put together then. A very hip friend of mine in the dorm, a girl who insisted on wearing sandals all winter, minus socks even, had done the same thing, searching through various publications—*Life* magazine, always a good bet—for pictures that would do the trick and make years of people and experience leap out of the wall with an electric, exuberant force. But it was doubly remarkable, there in the Sunderlands' bathroom. Because it was very cool, making one of those, a wall flooded with various cultural heroes, people off the grid inventing whole new grids. I was sure something odd and quirky remained in those Sunderlands after all, something of the rebel. Here was evidence. Maybe Ned was at the heart of that. At least, on the wall he was.

So when Kevin arrived—not an hour later, more like two—I didn't know what to expect. Frances was particularly unhelpful.

I know jack shit about the guy, she told me. I met him at our wedding. That's when I met her too. I only know Ned stayed with them here, and they bought him a bus ticket home. Oh yeah, in case you haven't guessed, they didn't like what he was doing either.

A bus ticket, I said, when was this? So he came home?

No, he didn't come home. He hung around the bus station a while, and cashed in that ticket. Then he hitched down to Big Sur. He called to tell me that about a week later. Eventually, they phoned me up—me, I hardly fucking knew them—and demanded I fill them in. I mean it was fairly obvious. Like, Ned wasn't back, right? He was still calling me from California. They got pissed. I know they'll bring up that stupid ticket again.

Frances had collapsed on the bed after her shower and putting on clean clothes; she was staring up at the ceiling. Big Sur, she said. That's one of our stops, you know. Hope that's okay.

Fine with me, I said, feeling a lot like Woody, fully up for the adventure. Then I worried I might be turning *into* Woody, being nice to strangers and all, acting responsible. Probably a midwestern thing. I'd have to watch that.

It's just *this* conversation, she added, here, with these guys. Let's say I'm steeling myself.

26

Frances! So Kevin burst into the room. I looked up to find—predictably—a fully straight looking guy in a pin-striped shirt, a suit, short hair. He had a little mustache—his concession to the world outside mostly falling apart—and he was taking off his jacket, loosening his tie, unbuttoning his collar.

It's so good to see you. He took a breath. I'm so sorry about Ned.

That sounded, on the face of it, like the bullshit everyone says. But the way Kevin got those two sentences out, I don't know. It seemed a heavy weight inside him connected to each word with the thinnest wire, about to break. Some badly jerry-built grief machine in there. Now the sight of Frances had kicked it on again. I felt sorry for both of them, even having to have this conversation.

Hi Kevin, Frances said gamely. What's going on?

Well, for one, dinner's going on. Joyce has made a feast for us. Come on.

And then we were walking down what we called in Chicago the *snake bladder* part of those old apartments, the narrow hallway that opened, by turns, into rooms and, at the end, one big widening which was, to the right, the start of a kitchen. Everything was gleaming in there, the light hitting their shiny toaster as Joyce smiled broadly, waving her dazzling metal spoon at us from the stove. With slow ceremony, she took off her apron and folded it carefully, smaller and smaller.

27

The four of us skipped the real dining room and ate in that kitchen. I can't remember quite what. A rice something, with peas. A fish something. Salad with greens I never saw before in my life, ultra curly ones, and bitter. Tomatoes like you'd get in Illinois but only in July or August, the fresh-picked time of year. Not in March. Certainly not in March. And chocolate cake. With whipped cream made from real cream, not the sort in an aerosol can that my brother would find in our mother's fridge and stand there in the open cold of it, pushing the little nozzle to the left, spraying that stuff straight into his mouth.

Frances hadn't said much. We were well into dessert now, and mainly they'd been spouting maudlin generalities about Ned. When that wasn't clogging the air, I'd been doing my job, chatting up those two, asking how they liked San Francisco—not *San Fran,* not *Frisco*—(they did, a lot), what their jobs were (Kevin: a corporate lawyer, but a ways away from making partner—not that I knew what that meant. And Joyce: a part-time secretary at a marketing firm but maybe occupational therapy—she'd have to go back to school for that—because it would be so much nicer to help people fix their problems, wouldn't it?). They showed zero interest in our trip, who had given us rides, how it looked, the brilliant early evening sun coming down on that endless, about-to-green-up-in-a-month-or-so prairie, all of it going sepia as day turned into night. And then those mountains. Just as well. I'd never be able to tell them. All of it would dissolve into what anyone would say. Finally, as Frances predicted, they got around to the business of the ticket.

I just can't believe Ned did that, said Joyce, his hugging us good-bye, watching us drive merrily off. And then stepping right up—he really did!—cashing that thing in for whatever it was. Almost a hundred dollars, wasn't it? I forget. She looked at Kevin.

Well, Joyce, that's water over the dam. We *are* so sorry about the accident, Frances, he said, facing her now and taking her hand. Such a loss. It must have been a terrible way to go. I hate to think about that moment, right before. I know he went straight down into a canyon, out there in Colorado.

So we all had to think about that moment again, that high ridge in the Rockies. Even me—who had never really pictured it before. I saw that red hair flying. I saw Ned frantic at the wheel, jamming the breaks, realizing in a sick flash how profoundly he'd fucked up.

Suddenly Frances looked up. So what happened to Ned, Kevin?

What do you mean?

It all flooded out of her then.

I want to know, she said, how did he seem here, what was he talking about? His state of mind, I mean. You knew him so long, Kevin. Can't you tell me one fucking real thing?

Here, she glanced at me. She was holding back tears. Then she straightened up, fearless.

Joyce started to say something, but Kevin held up his hand. Everything hovered there, in that kitchen. I could hear their clock—one of those great old Seth Thomas jobs—ticking away. I could hear people down in the street, one calling a dog, and kids laughing. After all, the windows were open, the weather perfect, about 65 degrees. It was suppertime, when everyone in the world is kicking back.

It's a very sad thing, Frances, he said. It really is.

What is?

How Ned was.

That's what I mean, Kevin. How *was* that?

The story began then and kept going. How Ned showed up on their doorstep, disoriented, talking gibberish. How he'd come down from Mill Valley where they really messed him up.

You two certainly must know how that is, Kevin said.

Sure, right, I thought. But it wasn't the moment to share that with Frances.

He claimed Ned's eyes didn't focus in the usual way. Maybe they were dilated too. Kevin couldn't remember. He was no doctor, of course, though it was clear that Ned kept staring straight at things, then doing double-takes, shaking his head.

Like maybe rattling his brains around? Like that would help? Joyce said lightly, tilting her head right and left in that stock loony way.

Joyce is just trying to lift the mood, Kevin said. But no one said a thing.

Well then, she went on between dainty bites of her chocolate cake. To be perfectly serious, Ned refused to eat a thing at first. But Frances, we insisted he sit down to three squares a day. That's the house rule, I told him. I just had to do that, didn't I, Kev? Lay down the law.

We gave him soup, Kevin said. Chicken, beef barley, mushroom, you know, Campbell's finest. He finally agreed to take some of that.

And saltines, Joyce added. But for a couple of days, he threw up nearly everything in the bathroom—and not *only* the bathroom. Such a mess! Well, I just have to say it—that was truly disgusting. We could *hear* him day and night. Good thing we never gave him anything with tomatoes in it. Oh god.

It was the drugs, Joyce, you know that. It was entirely a matter of those pills he was taking, said Kevin. He *was* taking pills, Frances. I'm afraid it wasn't just your normal everyday weed he was into anymore.

What kind of pills? said Frances.

Kevin shrugged. You think I know? Different—two or three colors. And sizes. Not that many, I guess. Of course we tried to take them away from him but he had hiding places. I didn't go through his stuff. That didn't seem right.

Ned had looked skinny. Kevin was certain he had lost weight since he'd seen him last. Not that he ever was a hulking type guy.

Yes, said Joyce, never *that,* recalling how he had tried out a couple of times for football in high school, Kevin already a star on that team called the *Barbs*—DeKalb the place where someone invented barbed wire—and was always told *no,* he never weighed enough though he was pretty fast, a good runner.

I tried to think that through, Ned even wanting to play football—such a taboo then to anyone on the other side of that countercultural divide. It seemed impossible, making that luminous, beautiful face stuck to the wall in the bathroom fit such a wish for violence and cheap triumph. A massive dumbing down. If true, remembering that must have been an embarrassment of staggering proportion to him.

And the gibberish? Frances asked. You said *gibberish* before. What was that about?

Your guess is as good as mine, said Kevin. He was talking the usual—excuse me—the usual drivel, you know. About karma and light years and who we were in the past and in the future, and how it was all happening at once. Blah blah blah. All that nonsense, that ridiculous talk about *being* and *who are we really?* and when we look, really look at things, what do we see; and color, why is blue *blue* and not red; and do we hear silence or sound the most? You know, stuff like *spaceship earth*—and here Kevin made a little sci-fi echoey sound as if to put it in quotations—that kind of thing, he said, what people like to dribble on and on about these days.

Well, *some* people, Joyce said. If it wasn't so heartbreaking, it would have been funny. Oh, and that hair of his. Really.

Her *really* hung there, clipped and sour, until Kevin looked up again.

It took us five full days to talk him into going home, back to Illinois, he said. By that point, Ned was eating okay, not sick anymore. He looked better.

You could say he perked up, Joyce said. He was starting to make sense, talking about *you,* Frances, about getting back to DeKalb.

What did he say about me? Frances said. It must have been a hard thing to ask.

Oh, I don't know. Like, how much he loved you. How much he liked being married. How really great you two were together. You know. She got that semi-moony sympathetic look.

Even Frances, as much as she wanted to believe that, must have seen this was Joyce spinning her wheels, making nice nice so in the story of the story she'd be one of the good guys. Or maybe she was just giving a sideways cue to Kevin about all the things she hoped he'd whisper in her ear.

Finally it seemed the right time to take him down to the bus station, Kevin said. We sprang for the ticket, of course. No problem, that. I mean, we have the money. But Ned seemed into the idea. He talked about the fascinating people he'd meet on the bus trip and whatnot. He was acting normal, close to normal anyway, and said something about seeing us at Christmas if we were coming back to visit the folks and all. I said we'd think about it. That we probably would. And Frances, believe me, he was very, very grateful to us.

Yes, that's right. And then it was just your normal bye-bye talk and everything, Joyce said. Who knew?

Who ever knows, I thought.

28

She is *such* a bitch, Frances said, such a grade A, fucking double-duty bitch and a half.

We were under our matching blue bedspreads, in that little guest room which we knew now to be on the other side of the apartment, the farthest point from the Sunderlands' bedroom. So it was safe to say such things. No one would hear us. It was late too, about 11:30 or so.

Not a bitch, I said. That word had been forbidden in our house. My mother's distaste for it had rubbed off on me. Anyway, *bitch* implied evil and planning and gravity. I wasn't sure Joyce deserved such credit. She's just vapid as hell, I said, a dyed-in-the-wool twit.

Yeah. She's not that smart. But way worse than that—she's a friggin' genius at being an idiot. She should get a prize or something.

Clearly, I said.

We both lay there, watching a fly intent on exploring the over-head light, which was turned off. But this was a city. You never got rid of that glow outside, seeping in. So we could still make things out.

You know what? They know nothing about Ned, Frances said. They don't. He's forever the bad boy to them, the fuck-up, the loser. I knew that *before* tonight. It's just a story to them. And flattering, really. It's like they did this social work on him or something and now they're so proud. He makes them feel better about themselves. Their shitty little empty selves.

Maybe, I said. But I think there's something in Kevin that gets what happened. Some little part of him anyway. I think he loved Ned.

Sure, he loved Ned. But that just means Ned loved *him.* And Kevin still feels that and has to give it back. These things hang on, you know. That's how it works with old friends.

What about that collage in the bathroom? Kevin did that, and that alone has to mean something.

The collage? You want to know who really fucking made that? Frances sat up now, looking fiercely at me.

Who?

Ned.

Ned? *What?*

Yeah, you were taking the plates over to the sink and stuff, talking to the twit. And I asked Kevin about that, I did.

And he said. . . .

He goes oh, that was Ned's project. His exact word for it: *project.* You know, like something you'd do in kindergarten. Only for Ned, it was "to get his head together" those four days he was here. That's what Kevin said. Frances put quotes around that phrase with her fingers like those Lincoln boys going on, sarcastic and giddy, about the great state of whatever, but she was darker about it, and angry. *Get his head together,* she repeated with acid all over it. Christ.

No way. I don't buy it. How could Ned put his big self up there, right in the middle of that wall? He was a pretty modest guy, wasn't he? That's like the ultimate egomaniac thing to do.

He *was* modest, said Frances. And shit, yeah, he would never never put himself up there. But that's the thing. He started up that circle of pictures, first doing the outer rim of it, moving in, adding person after person, toward the center.

And he never got there.

Fucking A, he never got there. All of a sudden they were taking him down to that shit-ass bus station. Honestly, they just wanted him out of here. So Ned left a big hole—for sure. And then Kevin colored up those eyes, the *wrong* color. He had taken that photo the first day, when Ned showed. And later, he blew it up and stuck it there, right in the middle. I can just see them, can't you? *Oh Kevin,* Joyce goes, *this is so cool.* Then he goes, *yeah Joyce, we're so creative!* I bet that's what all their friends told them too. *Cre-a-tive,* she said again, the word coming out of her with particular irony. It drifted there, in the window's dim light for a second.

Screw their grief or this being some tribute, Frances continued. It's all part of their goddamn good taste thing. They're just using Ned to show they're so hip and with-it, even though they're complete, 100 percent corporate sellout fucks.

There wasn't much to say after that. The small room grew immense, empty, even the poor fly at the end of something, circling up there, knocking himself senseless where ceiling met the wall.

A big hole, I said, trying to imagine Ned with scissors and glue, searching the pages of magazine after magazine, deepening into all those remarkable spirits, fixed on them, some still alive but others lost, under the sod: Martin Luther King, Robert Frost, John Lennon and Paul, Gandhi, Jane Addams, Dorothy Day.

Got that right, Frances said, a very big hole.

29

We were polite enough as we left the next morning. I said how good it was to meet them; I wished Kevin luck on making partner and hoped that Joyce would find some really dynamite occupational therapy program someplace close. I thanked them, of course. Joyce nodded, smiling. Kevin was smiling too, telling Frances to come back anytime. Whenever she wanted to talk about Ned, or any other thing for that matter. Where were we going now? he asked. But Frances wouldn't say. She told me later she didn't want their *vibes* coming after us. Staining us. Putting a bad trip on us. The whammy. The evil eye. He offered her fifty bucks but she shook her head.

We were, in fact, going up to Mill Valley, where Kevin claimed Ned had been truly screwed over. I sort of know some people there, Frances told me. But here is where my memory really breaks down—and probably my curiosity at the time. How did she know them? All of it was pretty sketchy to me, even then. But like Woody, I knew my place. I was—as my brother would say as a kind of mantra for years—*just happy to be here.*

And I *was* happy. I mean, we were in San Francisco—*Frisco, San Fran*—whatever you dared call it, which seemed the center of the world somehow, real *and* imagined. We walked west on Broadway, put our thumbs out and made our way down to the fabled Golden Gate Park, just outside of it, closer to the water. The ocean, here it was!—heaving and lying back endlessly, making its fantastic noise. The Sunderlands had given us a bag lunch. We found a pretty spot higher up, on a ridge, and by 10:30 we were digging into those sandwiches, watching little long-haired kids running around and various dogs on the loose too; people frolicking, playing Frisbee, panhandling, toking up; couples going at it; intent-looking sorts playing guitars and flutes even this early. One group down there, apparently doing nothing, sat in a circle, laughing wildly here at the start of the week, just a Tuesday. That was an LSD thing, I thought, or a mescaline thing where, with luck, they wouldn't need to move a muscle to be intricately entertained for hours.

I don't know why I'm on this bullshit trip, said Frances suddenly, looking out into the water which was mindless, which wouldn't quit moving until it hit China. It's colossally stupid, you know? And depressing as hell. Dismal.

About Ned, you mean?

The who-he-was part, she said. Like, I know the part I knew. But what am I supposed to do with that crap from those two last night? Kevin and Joyce. This is so awful. Poor Ned. Jesus. What friends. Great. *Perk up! Give him soup!* Oh, I don't know.

I didn't feel like defending the Sunderlands. But I remembered something.

I can tell you a story.

Frances lay back in the grass. Why not? she said, closing her eyes. Shoot.

30

It wasn't a *story* story since it actually happened. *In real life,* as they say. But I started anyway in that vein because that's what memory does. So the brain can pick up what took place once and carry it other places. So the mouth can find words for it. So it gains weight and casts a shadow. It's an illusion that a thing has a beginning and an end, that something not utterly pointless runs through it. Some reason. Or maybe just one person breathing. You breathe—no big deal—as you're telling a story, bringing some bit of your life back so oxygen gets in. The red blood cells light up. But really it's dark there, not a speck of daylight or moonlight and what we think is bright red is actually worlds quieter and stranger, a blue we'll never know the color of, locked in the past of that body.

Anyway, I saw this sign last fall, I said. To go caving. And I thought that would be cool.

See, Frances said with her eyes still closed, Mr. Lutowski was right. We should have gone to Hannibal.

Yeah, I suppose. But it seemed exciting, you know? The *idea* of mucking about in a cave. So I called the number on the sign— this was at school, it was a university club. They said, sure, show up and you're in. No sandals. Wear decent shoes. We have the other stuff.

I went on, making a short story longer as my mother would say, my mother who loved to screw up clichés just enough so they'd still be recognizable. I told Frances how I talked my roommate Nell into coming and this boy in my history class, tall, skinny Greg, painfully awkward, who always sat next to me with nothing to say. Wanna go caving? I asked him. He nodded. And he showed up too. That's pretty much all I know about him still. That he was willing, and that he did.

So we piled into a car, two cars, early that morning. Maybe eight or nine of us, including two full-of-themselves sorts who ran the thing, who seemed to be our leaders, holding forth on various caves en route, fighting in the car about which one we might go to as we drove south and west into Missouri, cave capital of the U.S., it turns out. Like, the whole state has a basement and sub-basement, tunnels and mountains down there, much of it never explored. So I guess we did have a lot of options. Forget that back in Champaign people thought we were going—no getting out of it—to one specific already decided place. Because we changed course in the car. I mean our two fearless leaders—Jeff and Maria—changed *their* minds and we ended up, three hours later, at a bent and battered garbage can lid just lying there, in an old bean field. It was October, everything picked and cut back. No farmer in sight. Late morning by then.

Where's the damn cave? Nell said, my roommate Nell, who would never quite forgive me. We were putting on these helmets. Each had a soft lick of flame jetting out in front, once you lit it. I never learned what they were called. But you could put your hand right through that fire and it wasn't hot. It wasn't even that warm.

One of the leaders—Maria—stepped forward and lifted the garbage can lid. We stared at the man-size circle of darkness there on the ground. That was hole we would enter. That was the cave.

It's called *vertical climbing,* the first part, Maria told us. She had this deadpan voice. Okay, campers, she said, hop in. Now drop.

31

Was I boring Frances to smithereens? What was I telling this for? Off shore, out on the ocean, I saw ships. I saw men shrunk by distance pulling on ropes, some just standing on deck. I guessed they were smoking cigarettes, dreaming off, taking a break. So I stopped too.

Frances opened her eyes. So what the fuck happened next? she said. That's not *it,* is it?

No.

Shit. You actually did it? You went down that hole? Shit and a half, I would have been out of there.

What? You kidding? And sit in the car in the middle of bean-field-nowhere for eight hours, waiting? That was the only alternative. But believe me, it did run through my head.

So Frances closed her eyes again and I kept on with my story, how we all took turns and lowered ourselves down, into that ladder-like descent. Into that honest-to-zeus underworld. And slid down and caught ourselves on stony footings, then slid, then caught until—whoa! we were there, *rock bottom* for real. And a massive room opened up. A whole mountain range, miles of it. I'd never seen anything so astonishing in my life.

Hey, it was dark down there, right? Frances had turned on her side, propped up on one elbow. What I mean is, how could you see anything?

Those helmets and their flames, I said. They cast pretty good light, especially when we got behind each other in a wobbly, half-assed sort of order and started climbing those mountains, all dark, but it was glorious and bizarre, kind of heart-stopping. You could see this line of lights ahead of you, one by one strung out along the high ridge as we moved forward. Like we were one big linked animal or something. Really, it's an entire universe down there.

Like, mainly you just hiked, like in some ordinary state park? Frances said. I knew she was thinking of Starved Rock in Illinois or Turkey Run in Indiana, each with its canyons and ravines the glacier once rooted up everything to make and leave there, by way of its ancient drag and spill.

Yeah, mostly. Only we were really down there. It was dark, so everything had this eerie, surreal ghost thing about it. Not all of it was mountain range. Sometimes the trail—if you can call it that—would thin out, rock face close on either side and we'd be inching along some endless, small passage, forcing ourselves through openings and under outcroppings you wouldn't believe. And life down there too.

You mean, like creatures?

I mean like the smallest frogs, and ultra cool little crawdad guys in the water which pooled out in places. Only the thing is, because of the darkness, they're all translucent. You could see right through their skin or whatever it's called. You could see their organs, fluids moving in there, flashing from one to another, tiny little hearts beating.

That's damn cool, Frances said.

Damn right it was damn cool. But after three or four hours, Maria and Jeff said, okay guys, let's turn back. So we did. But that's when the trouble began.

Don't tell me.

Yeah, see, I guess it was raining outside. And apparently that changes the *look* of the cave, inside.

You got lost.

Lost? We got seriously, death-knell lost. Then it was Jeff and Maria, those lunatics, fighting every second: how did we come, this way or that? This narrow passage or what? Like, this right turn or straight ahead? Yeah, well, so much for leaders, right? The rest of us stood around, soaked now, plastered with mud, popping lemon drops.

Lemon drops?

That was the other thing. We had no food, not much water. I guess they had counted on a three or four hour hike, max. I told you, they were total dimwits.

But you're here, Frances said. Obviously you got out.

Sure, we got out. But that was an accident, pure luck. Really, an out-and-out miracle. We basically kept walking—that kept us warm—saying sometimes how yes, that ledge looks familiar or yeah, I remember that little pool, that streambed. But it was all horseshit. Room after room down there, it all began to look the same. And then someone pointed out that no one back at the university even knew we were in *this* particular cave. So then it happened.

What?

It began to sink in: we'd never be found.

32

I figure not many people my age then, ones I knew anyway, had had such a moment, sure they were done for, over, *kaput,* though of course Woody had plenty of that from his time as a medic. As I told my story to Frances, I realized I hadn't thought about it much. It rattled me to put it out there, in the air like that.

So you had this bunch of people who all thought they were dead meat? Interesting, she said.

Frances was trying to picture it. I don't think I was doing a very good job at helping her. It was a little difficult, given where we were, up on that ridge overlooking the vast blue Pacific, one of the most lovely spots on earth. That's the trouble with a place like California. It ruins you for calamity. For complexity.

It got way past interesting, I told her, thinking how each of us sucked in this news, that we might never get out of that cave, never go back to Illinois, how it fell through us, that we—the motley few of us there—might be the last human beings we'd ever see, stuck by this terrible turn of events. That we'd die slowly together.

I bet some of them starting bawling their eyes out too, Frances said.

Maybe. I don't know, I said and then went quiet myself. How to tell her? Because that's the odd part. There was this hopeful thing and it sort of changed shape as we walked. Sometimes you could work it up bigger, take a bellows to it. Sometimes it got really little, hand-sized then, at best it might balance on the tip of your finger. But it got smaller and smaller. Sometimes it blinked right out.

Hey, so then what? said Frances.

Some did start crying, you're right, I told her. Others kept joking, dumb jokes like promising we'd see a McDonald's just around the bend or something. Like, oh man, we'd be laying our teeth into a juicy old cheeseburger in a minute or two. They were the best sorts to have along though the jokes were bad, not jokes at all, I guess. We got pretty goofy, stupid-goofy. Some people went hysterical. Or dead quiet, like Greg, that poor guy from my history class. But he was practically mute to begin with; he just got muter. I was surprised at what happened to me.

You got hysterical, I bet.

At first, sort of. I felt this panic begin to rise in me. And rise. And rise. And then I got all reasonable, like, I'm only 20. What the hell. I'm not married, I don't have a kid. There's no one depending on me. This is probably all right. Nobody will miss me for long. And then I was okay with it. I really was.

You're kidding. That *is* weird.

Well, it was weird. But there it is. We kept walking anyway.

And you got out finally.

Yeah, finally. We were all dragging along, hungry, pretty chilled, and we felt something in the air. A rush, a sudden different kind of something. Cooler, newer air, with the smell of trees in it or old vegetation, something sweet and rotting. We looked up and saw the hole. *The* hole. And man, we were up that sucker in a flash.

Whoa, that's way trippy, said Frances.

What I remember most, I told her, was the second I came out of there, when half of me was still sunk in the hole. It was night by then. That's how long we were in that cave. It was raining like mad. I could make out a very thin line of trees, like something inked in then blurred by a brush, and the sky just a lighter shade of the same dark color the earth was. Nothing impressive, not the sort of thing anyone in their right mind would want to paint.

But shit, there it was, Frances, the most fucking beautiful field of my life. There it was, I heard myself say again, like someone else was whispering those words to me.

33

We just sat there for a while, a few minutes at least. The people in a circle below, the ones who had probably downed some mescaline, were silent too, a couple or so hunched over, studying blades of grass, others lying back, staring with great attention into the leafy shade. I remember doing exactly that once, outside of Champaign in Allerton Park.

Well, Frances said, quite a story. Remind me never to go caving.

I'm sorry, I said. I guess it was a dumb thing to go on and on about.

I understood she was in a better state of mind now though I couldn't think *why* I even told that story, why I thought it might answer something. It did have a semi-happy ending. Maybe that was it. As we liked to say later about any scary, unsettling movie that finally turns out okay, locked in a gladder place: it was pure Jane Austen.

No, it was good to hear that, she said. I'm into those fucking hopeless cases, the ones where all the parts come together at the end. I liked how you felt that wind, and smelled it. Trees and shit out there you couldn't see yet. I guess sometimes it really is like that.

But I couldn't stop. We never had a clue, I said, as if it needed a postscript, some big P.S. to underscore something. A surprise, a complete accident that we ever got out, I added needlessly. And kept sputtering like I couldn't give it up, so kept saying these lame things. Because I wanted to stay in that terrible story, keep figuring what really happened down there in that netherworld. It was Frances who saved me from myself, changing the subject.

Look, we better split. We better hit the road.

So it's Mill Valley, I said as Frances stood up, lifting her pack into place.

34

It took us almost no time, just over the Golden Gate Bridge, past Sausalito and Marin City and then we went west at a place called Strawberry Point. Two rides. We were back in regular cars again, no van, just the driver each time.

First, some woman who swore she'd swum the English Channel—I could see she'd told her story a hundred times, her details that rich and *accumulated,* it seems right to say. All about what kind of fish she saw—angel fish followed her the whole time, like little puppies—and the waves, which weren't bad those three days. Trust me, she said. But neither Frances nor I believed a word though we admired her invention.

Then some hippie guy named River-Run took us straight into Mill Valley. He was a carpenter, he said, and from that city so named because it was, for over a century, the place the giant redwoods were taken to be, well, *milled,* hence *Mill Valley.* Get it? he asked as if that particular two plus two was a matter of rocket science. He seemed proud of what he did, complaining that everyone and his brother thought they could be carpenters now, making their know-nothing dumbfuck claims to know something. Because it was the ultimate hip thing to do, to work with your hands, wasn't it? He said that—*work with your hands*—like it was big-time sacred stuff. But he was the real thing. He knew from wood—the difference between cedar and oak and pine. Total crap, that pine. Better for crates really. I thought of those skinny, needley trees that tower over us, falling in sacrifice to box up oranges and lemons, eventually to do time as an end table at the side of some ratty couch, to hold up a bubbling lava lamp when the real lights went off. I sat up front both times, the appointed liaison with the great world now that we'd lost Woody.

River-Run dropped us where Frances told him. It felt a little. . . . *suburbo,* we called such a place. My mother would have claimed that simply more of my reverse snobbery at work. But here were rows of compact largely look-alike houses, howbeit different paint jobs, with their middle-sized lawns, their flowering trees—magnolia, plum, cherry—all on the smallish size too, set just so. In a couple of hours, some mom would no doubt be rushing out the door, her son in tow who would be dragging his baseball gear in a canvas bag, getting in the car to head out for after-school practice. But no, Frances insisted, this was one cool neighborhood. Just watch.

We walked up the walk of a place with a picket fence, a porch, music blaring inside—Janis Joplin—set to the highest possible decibel so I knew we'd be shouting.

Who are these people? I did shout, right into Frances's left ear.

Friends of Ned. Who the friggin' else would they be? she yelled back though the music abruptly turned off now, leaving her last few words hanging loudly in the air by themselves. A guy stood smiling at the door and I could see several others inside, sitting in a circle. They were passing a joint around.

No one seemed to recognize Frances. That appeared not to matter. The guy at the door welcomed us, and the others, moving over, offered us a seat in their circle. I think most were guys but I can't be sure about that. They were all smiling at us now until the music came on again, this time the Grateful Dead as background, kept low. A few were in white robes, some in colorful strings of beads looped many times around their necks, others wearing tie-dyed kerchiefs there or the ordinary cowpoke kind, just the thing to put on dogs too, where a collar should be. A couple of them sat cross-legged in full overalls, no shirts, others in beat-up jeans and turtlenecks. They were saying things to no one in particular like *oh yeah man,* like *yeah, like I dig it,* letting the music take them somewhere. Now and then, when our turn with the joint came, Frances and I did that heaving in and holding smoke thing, letting it seep out. We hadn't said anything. Early afternoon, the air choked with drifts of incense and marijuana. Some of them started to talk then. To be puzzled about us.

Where you chicks from? one of the overall guys said slowly, so slowly those words hardly seemed in the same sentence. Nearly everyone was looking toward us again.

Illinois, said Frances just like earlier, in that old beatnik-turned-hippie van. The room felt smaller. In the background, we were told how we should come, hear, Uncle John's band, over and over again, those subtle liquid harmonies the Grateful Dead were famous for. It's like you could lie down on those sounds, like they were the thickest water you could float in and happily get nowhere at all, watching fish dive and dart and flash by. The perfect soundtrack, I thought, for that English Channel wannabe. She should check it out.

Illinois: the circle took in this fact. So that was floating too. They seemed to be making sense of it. And maybe some of them had been—absolutely—to Chicago once.

Wow, Illinois, said one of the turtlenecks. Then he turned to the robe next to him who had his eyes closed and was doing that *om* thing, but you could barely hear it. Hey Shashee, you know that guy who was here before, that fucking brilliant cat who talked all that mind-blowing shit? Wasn't he from Illinois?

No answer from the robe.

Yeah, came a voice from the circle's other side, fucking into Heidegger. And Zen, like that. Yeah. And wasn't it De-something he was from, there in Illinois? DeWit? DeYork? DeWhatever it was? It was too much. The town would never be found.

Let's see, said the guy who'd been at the door. From Illinois, yeah, and his name was. . . . He stopped there, drifting off, but Jerry Garcia was still at it, doing something behind all of us, no end in sight for that layering up and water-life.

Ned! said someone to my left in his tie-dyed everything, just like the Lincoln boy. Yeah, and that nifty thing he did with the tree, remember? Cooler than shit, man.

Yes yes, Ned. Far out! I dug that guy, yeah, said one of the robes, not the one with closed eyes. Fuck, yeah. *Ned*! He was a full-tilt genius. Swear on my mother's grave!

I'd never heard that expression: *full-tilt genius.* Or the second one either, *on my mother's grave,* truly a figure of speech, given that their mothers—I think this now—were probably in their late 40s, early 50s, no doubt mostly suburban moms fully alive that moment, heading off to lunch somewhere *nice,* a couple of them wondering now and then where their boys were and quickly repressing the thought.

Any chance you two know him? A long shot, that's true, said the door guy, coming alert again. Right! Ned. . . . he said once more. Where is it in Illinois you from? You know him?

It was Frances's turn with the joint. She took a long drag, then slowly let it out. She stared around the circle like she was savoring each face, one by one by one. It was her moment to be far and away brilliant, with that timing.

Yeah, she said, Ned was my husband.

35

It freaked them out, big time. Frances had style. She could knock people flat. First that poor thoughtless woman in the hippie-beatnik van. Now these guys, who were a mixed-up bunch, that's for sure. But they had at least one thing in common: they revered Ned. Now they remembered it all. They did think he was a regular Einstein. He had told them things.

Things like: You can live forever and ever if you choose.

Things like: I can teach you to fly. It's all in the small of the back.

Things like: Dreams are the only real thing. You're only dreaming that you're awake.

Things like: You can come back from the dead, if you want to.

Things like: But who would want to? Just look at this world.

Somehow those guys knew about the accident. They were all over Frances about that. And sincere. What a fucking waste, they said. But probably there was a reason, they said. He'd clearly be reborn immediately at a higher level and do fantastic shit in the next life. What level or life that was, not one of them seemed to know. I flashed on the nearly luminous see-through frog in that cave then, deep down, below Missouri. The smallest of those frogs, its tiny lungs billowing out, filling up, then giving it all back to the dark. That would work for me, next time I had a chance.

The thing is, it seemed those guys were positive for a couple of hours that Frances *was* Ned in some time-travel, jump-the-River-Styx sort of way. Or at least she could channel him, had been sent to continue the conversation he started with them. Pretty soon though, they discovered she knew almost nothing about William James or Zen koans or the proper breathing pattern for some fancy, ancient, recently-discovered-in-the-west yoga posture. And no matter how much dope they smoked, apparently nothing in Frances's words quite echoed the way Ned could repeat a fairly mundane statement like *this cup has a blue handle, doesn't it?* or *you know, a window is made of both glass and wood* until it belonged in the Garden of Eden, weighted and glowing there—anyone could see it—next to the apple, before the snake got to it.

I knew exactly what was going on since it had happened to me the summer I graduated from high school. This fall from grace. This *kind of, not really* fall from grace. This one big fat reality check.

36

In my case, it was just your run-of-the mill basement, at the edge of Chicago. And my best friend, Jill Zonik, was eager to get high. But *naturally,* she cautioned. Not by smoking a joint. None of that.

Since we had no dope and no idea at all how to get any, this seemed a plausible alternative. But how? I said. How in the world do we do that?

She had read it somewhere. You do it through tapes—reel to reel, or maybe use a tape deck—through unlikely sounds, something recorded. There'd be a lot of repetition and flat-out boring stuff you'd hear, maybe a ton of chanting too until basically you'd blank out, your mind leaving your body, maybe in self-defense. What was left in your skull, where your brain had been—that emptiness come to life—would tell you things. Amazing things. And that void would tune you into the history of the universe, where we'd been and where we'd end up, all that, everything. Voila: natural high. A real trip.

But we had no tapes either. None like that. It was a major problem but Jill wasn't deterred. She did have a record, she said. It was her father's, and weird, so maybe it would fill the bill. I said to her on the phone, bring it over. We have this little Oriental rug down in the basement. We can sit cross-legged on that, just like you're supposed to. My mother won't notice a thing.

This was late July 1968, a month before we both went off to college, the summer *after* the famous Summer of Love in San Francisco. My high school boyfriend—not a little inflated, that phrase, for my one date, a fix-up that spring for the prom we weren't allowed to call a prom—was one Nikos Stephanopoulos, who turned out to be the most drop-dead beautiful boy at that dance. Nikos—Nick at times, or even Nicky—who stunned all the girls down to their two-inch heels when we walked into the place. How did *you* get *him?* my friends asked me in the john that night, genuinely impressed. He is *so* cute, they said. And what a name!

Nick—or Nikos—however gorgeous, was easy to be around, unassuming. I mean, he was nice enough to take me to my own prom, pretty much a setup, a blind date, having met me only briefly through mutual friends about a week before. But he had wanderlust. He had heard about Haight-Ashbury, knew all about the earlier Summer of Love. His father had made him work through those months in the family's candy shop though he passionately wanted to get out there. Surely there'd be a second Summer of Love, he said, so he could. *Newsweek* read like a travel brochure for the first one; he still carried that issue around with him.

But it was curious. He didn't look the part. Nick had one of those early Beatles haircuts, the mophead kind, about three years too late. Clean-cut, sweet, clearly smart, he had a trusting, fearless look. Even my towering, ultra-intimidating Aunt Virginia, a high school principal and not easily smitten by anyone, had nodded in slow approval when she saw the pictures from that dance, the two of us awkward and smiling, me in a long dress, Nick—yes, unbelievably endearing—in his white tux, a moment my mother clicked into the photo frieze of being young forever. But he wanted to see the world for himself. No second Summer of Love, not really, but he had taken off to California, had vanished, had been swallowed up regardless.

Meanwhile, Jill and I diligently set ourselves up in my basement for our own transcendental experience. We had the record player out; we had the record. We were fully poised to *om* to it, sitting just so, cross-legged, closing our eyes, our hands resting in place on our bent knees, making that circle with thumb and forefinger we'd seen in pictures of the Maharishi meditating. Beyond ready, we were *primed:* to lift out of our heads into whatever ecstasy might be available or short of that, whatever wisdom. But first, Jill leapt up to switch the phonograph on and lower its arm, hurrying back to her place next to me on the small carpet.

And—what kind of record? Odd, yes. Jill was dead-on about that. But what possessed her father to have such a thing? It turned out to be an unfathomable litany of sound effects—hammers hammering, trucks backfiring, seawash on some shore, a hawk doing its high, straight-down nose dive attack call, an oncoming train, eggs cracking, water running, a wolf in the long distance, a razor taking out a beard slowly, scraping over skin, a loon calling, someone eating popcorn, one sloppy, buttery kernel after another, on and on and on, all rushing over us, needling us, the whole thing annoying beyond belief as we tried doggedly to leave our bodies behind and go anywhere else.

It was exactly this moment that we heard the basement door open—seemingly just another sound effect. But it was my mother shouting down to us.

Nick is here! Your friend Nicky, come back from California!

I opened my eyes, caught half-*oming* between the hawk attack and the eggs breaking on the side of a cup, to see Nikos Stephanopoulos walking like a god down the stairs, his thick black beard and long black hair, his full white robe. He was smiling. He was carrying *The Tibetan Book of the Dead*.

No, Frances couldn't be Ned. It wasn't going to happen.

37

Hey, you know what else? They're into some weird shit around here, Frances whispered to me out in the yard later. We were each spooning down a deep bowl of rice and lentils, and there was homemade bread, rich with seeds and wheat berries. I never saw a wheat berry before. I figured that's what wheat was before someone crushed it screaming to death. Well, not screaming. I'm sure it went quietly.

It's not that they don't love Ned and everything, Frances said.

That was some relief to her after hearing Kevin and Joyce go on in their tisk-tisk oppressive way.

I just don't know about these guys, she added. I mean, they mean well.

And the ways they loved Ned were pretty evident. One thing was the tree business, famous now, if you count how many times they kept mentioning it. In fact, Ned had dressed one up, a smaller one, a flowering plum. This was before anyone much thought of TPing anything, for whatever reason, at least in the Midwest. But he had taken crepe paper, all colors of it, and woven up that tree to great glory. He had dyed marshmallows green and blue and red and yellow—colors of those Mt. Everest Tibetan flags—and hung those about, sometimes attached to yarn. He had made the tree a giant symbol. Of what, no one was actually sure. But those guys practically worshiped it. They left offerings of oranges and bread and chocolate near where its roots bolted up out of the ground a little. And did some serious chanting before it most evenings, right there in the yard. Eventually, the rain did a number on it—all that soggy crepe paper, the dyes from it running into the grass—but that took a while. Not many storms out there, I guess. In certain seasons anyway.

Did you hear their latest scheme? Frances said. They're building a boat.

38

When I look at a map now, I can see Mill Valley is only a couple of miles or so from the coast though not Sausalito, not Tiburon, both right on the water. It's inland, not terribly far if you compare it to anything really landlocked, like Illinois, for instance—if you don't count Lake Michigan. But even that little way in from the shore surprises me given how those guys talked that evening and the next morning; you'd think you could drag any seagoing vessel down easy, to blue water. It would take about, oh, two minutes. And yes, they were building a boat. Frances was on target.

Yeah, but get this. This will blow you away, she said. The reason. *Why* they're building one.

Lay it on me, I said, finishing up the last spoonful of the lentil-rice whatever it was.

They have this guru.

Okay, they have this guru. Big deal. It's common practice out here, isn't it?

But he's an old guy, said Frances. He's about to pack it in.

You mean, die?

Yes, die. Give up the ghost.

So? What's the point of the boat then? Are these guys taking him into the afterlife themselves?

That wouldn't surprise me, at least them *thinking* they could manage such a thing. I'd read a lot of Greek myth earlier that year, in a class I took at Illinois. I knew about Charon and the smoky river he crosses with every recent ex-resident of this sad world, going into the next one over that water, with his giant-size oar. And Charon makes an appearance at the end of one of my favorite Allen Ginsberg poems too, the one about the supermarket where Walt Whitman's in produce, hovering over the peaches and oranges, permanently on record "eyeing the grocery boy."

Well, sort of the afterlife, I guess, Frances said. But no, not yet. This will happen *before* either of them kicks off. It's just that he, *their* old guru, has never met *his* guru. Who lives in Peru, by the way.

Peru? You mean South America? But how can he have a guru he's never met, even if he's a guru himself? That makes no sense at all.

It does make sense. Because, see, *their* guru has met *his* own guru a lot. But only on an astral plane. Not in real everyday life.

What? Some out-of-body thing? Is that what you're saying?

I was waving my hands high then, staring at the sky as if that would explain anything. Maybe it was dreaming they meant, that those two only met in dreams and now finally wanted a waking moment to themselves, face to face. I could almost buy that. It *was* sort of sweet.

Frances moved closer. Who knows? This is the kind of thing Ned could talk hours about. The point is this connection, get it? Guru meets guru at last, or something. And they're going to all this trouble to make it happen. That part's cool, don't you think? Almost a love story. It's damn nice of these guys, to want to bring these two old oldies together. In the flesh. Before one of them, you know, dies.

But South America's a long way from here. Think about it, Frances. Making a boat is cuckoo enough. And then, there's the getting there. To friggin' Peru? Are they serious? Like, do these guys even know how to sail a boat like that? You have to know maps and currents, navigation crap, how to bail when the leaks start. It's probably endless, the stuff you need to know. These guys don't even *look* the part.

The men on those ships, the ones we saw out in the water near Golden Gate Park smoking their cigarettes, I thought of them. How tough they had seemed, weather-worn, beat to all get-out. You could spot that, even from a distance. There was a reason they looked that way. It was doubtful that this circle of dreamy weed-smoking good hearts could pull off such a trip, no matter how well intentioned.

Seems a little flippy to me, I said as quietly as I could manage. And maybe not a little, I added.

But there's more. Frances lowered her voice too. Something way flippier and why I'm telling you. Their plan's gotten bigger since we came today. It includes you and me now.

39

Once those guys decided that Frances wasn't exactly Ned, not even close, I guess they refocused on their more immediate reason to stay alive: to build that boat, to take Satamanyu, their guru, to see his guru down in Peru. Ned had met their guru once or twice and had approved. Which is what the guy who had first stood at the door told us later that afternoon, before letting it out that his name was Mukunda, not his original given one. I'm fairly certain that had been ordinary, like Phil or Brian. This *Mukunda* thing was a christening he brought on himself in a moment of dazzling realization he said he had no words to describe. Or maybe Satamanyu named him, who knows.

A Brian morphing into *Mukunda,* and *Shashee* probably once first and foremost Steve: that naming, that *renaming* was a curious habit that hung on, full force, for at least a decade. Later, in the early '80s, my husband and I, back from two years of teaching in Taiwan and getting our bearings in America again, would stay for a while at a co-op in Wisconsin, Madison's Netherwood Co-op, a lovely old fraternity house on Lake Mendota sold in the late '60s because who in his right mind wanted to be in a frat when the whole world-as-we-knew-it was dissolving, blowing up, and coming back new? Among the more standardly named residents at Netherwood—plain old Gail and Bill and Liz, sometimes Callaghan or *hey, Sealock!*—lived a young woman who called herself

Starfish (nee Nancy), a guy named *Seeker* (born Kenneth), *Kiva* (a former Edwin), *Mika* (first a Linda), and *Spoon* for whatever dubious reason (previously Duane).

One of the house members turned out to be a middle-aged Chinese scientist. *Mr. Ts'ou,* my husband always respectfully addressed him though others in that place called him *Joe,* not bothering to learn the exact pronunciation, thinking—no matter how we explained otherwise—that the ubiquitous surname *Ts'ou* was his given name, that anyway he liked being called Joe, more American sounding, as if he'd been awarded *most improved player* on the bowling team. In truth, he'd recently arrived to study physics at the university, jubilant in his quiet way, so relieved to be sprung from the days of the Cultural Revolution where he had been sent to the backest backwater to slop pigs for a time. For all we knew, as a smarty-pants educated sort, already with two degrees, Mr. Ts'ou was one of the guys wearing those tall white dunce caps in the famous photographs, Mao showing the intelligentsia what was what and who was really who. In Madison, he was always asking us questions like the one that slipped out of him as we walked near the Student Union, amused at the ducks that dotted the lawn, their gadding about for a stray potato chip from someone's lunch.

Who owns these ducks? Mr. Ts'ou had asked.

No one, I said. They just live out here, near the water.

Can we eat them?

As for the name changing and identity ratcheting-up at Netherwood, he had an equally simple question, whispered urgently to us one afternoon when no one else was afoot in the house.

What laws have they broken? he asked in Chinese, then slowly, more carefully in English.

As for now, for *here* in Mill Valley, it was Mukunda perfectly urgent about everything—including his name—as deliberate as Mr. Ts'ou would be but bowing his head when he talked to us, especially to Frances. A little of the oldest-time religion in that. Yet like a lot of those guys, his language hadn't changed much to match his new lofty state or name. It was still mainly *shit, yeah* and *I dig it* and *fuck, no way, man* when any conversation really got going. And shit, yeah, Ned thought their guru Satamanyu very cool indeed. Mukunda said so. Then he was bowing a million times, as if to underscore that fact.

Like I said, a genuinely mixed-up bunch. Frances was right. They *were* hard to pin down. Because every one of them would flip from the offhand, swear-enriched colloquial model to speak formally, funny-formal on occasion, these Americans, as if what they said was a translation, or some skewed pidgin English.

We are most happy in this hour to have you among us, Mukunda said at last, coming up from bow number whatever.

40

It would be a long journey by sea. Their boat was almost finished. We could see it sticking out of the garage, its wooden keel about nine feet high, practically an ark. It barely cleared the roof beam. And when a little subcommittee of them found us that evening, they popped the question formally. Though Frances had gotten the drift earlier that something was up, she knew nothing of the details.

We have this idea, said one of the robes, the one who had kept his eyes closed earlier, the one called Shashee. He seemed to be the spokesman at present, now that his sight had been restored.

It was easy for us to look blank and say nothing. That seemed the polite thing to do, a way of acknowledging our total attention to whatever they might say.

We're building a boat. Maybe you noticed it, in the garage.

We nodded dutifully. Who could miss it?

Well, Frances, you know the reason for that boat, yes? And you've told your friend here? How it concerns our beloved Satamanyu? Perhaps you both have spoken earlier about these matters with Mukunda.

Sort of, Frances said. I mean, yeah. About your guru's own personal guru, and the trip to Peru, the astral plane and everything? Sure, we're both hip to that.

Everyone in the group smiled at us. We could have basked in that if we wanted to, like turtles piled up on a river log some bright spring day. But they stalled out for the moment, maybe working up the nerve to hit the next level of our chat. I could hear them breathing.

Okay, I'll cut to the chase then, Shashee said. The fact is we have seen and measured your inner goodness. Both your auras passed the test with flying colors.

Yeah, said another one of the robes, we mean literally. Your auras are violet and gold. That means joy and compassion, which is very far out news.

And some blue and turquoise in there too, said a turtleneck. That's enthusiasm, meaning you're *into* stuff, in a good way. And humor. Like, you're funny too.

The point is, well, this is an invitation, said Shashee. We want you girls to come with us. To Peru.

Now they were the ones nodding. The small group moved toward us, closing in.

Go with you? What? I said. In that boat? Why? I mean, what for?

It was getting a bit more than strange though I was curious for a half-second about my aura. Joy and compassion? Right. *If these guys only knew us,* I thought. But that aura business. I flashed on those old boxy x-ray machines in shoe stores when I was a child, the ones with three pairs of binocular-like eye-holes, one for the salesman, one for your mom, and one built into the side of the thing, closer to the floor for the much shorter *kid*-you to peer at your feet and see the intricate bones lit up down there. I imagined getting at an aura was something close to that. And equally surprising. I wondered what mine looked like, its shape, now that they had filled us in on the color scheme. Maybe like my head set on fire, or maybe just my hair flaring up, everything ghostly and reversed, as in a black-and-white negative.

We think, Shashee said slowly. No, strike that. We *know,* and have come to the happy conclusion that you two chicks would be groovy cooks on our voyage.

I glanced at Frances, relieved that at least these guys weren't white slavers in the sex trade or anything. They were definitely aiming for a higher plane; not a surprise since virtually all of them seemed curiously asexual, somehow beyond such earthy concerns. Still, I suspected that since they were sure now that neither of us—Frances, and certainly not me—was the philosopher king Ned had been, and both from the hinterlands where women still wore aprons and canned rhubarb and cheerfully welcomed their kind home from school each day, that we'd be good bets for this. Fact: they would need to eat on the trip. Fact: someone had to cook the stews, bake the bread, the sweet-somethings for dessert. Fact: females automatically knew how to do those things, didn't they? Especially females of our ilk, from the far away middle of the country where no one was very cool yet—maybe *not ever*—so still attended to stuff like that. They didn't exactly say this but Frances and I could read their minds. We were getting good at it.

Now the whole lot of them was nodding and bowing. And smiling again, fully confident that we would enthusiastically agree. We'd understand their invitation as the great honor it was.

We want you to come with us, Shashee said again. Very much. All of us. Here he made a sweeping gesture with both arms.

As a tribute to Ned, he added reverently, bowing again in the most exaggerated way.

41

That last move—a tad sleazy, I have to say, their pandering that way, invoking Ned in their argument. Crazy, the entire thing. Not to mention the fact that Frances and I knew beans about cooking. Of course, that's what we'd mostly be making: lentils and great northerns and the red and black variety, grains too, barley and rice and noodles, and yes, wheat berries, stuff that would store well on such a trip. I had learned that much. But those old jokes about not knowing how to boil water? That was me, for sure. That was, apparently, Frances too, if you could judge the way she looked at Shashee, dumbfounded, like she didn't know English, like she didn't quite understand what he had said.

But I don't know shit from shinola about cooking, she blurted out. Do you? She had turned to me.

Nope, not me, I said. And I pictured Jack standing at the stove that morning he introduced me to Frances, pushing onions around, knowing just how long to keep that flame on high, then on medium, then completely off. He'd think this hysterically funny.

Believe me, Frances said, Ned wouldn't want *me* cooking on any trip. He hated my food, I swear on a Bible. You guys would all starve. Or I'd poison you. Not on purpose, of course, she added.

They looked extremely perplexed. How could this perfect plan not work?

We'll have to consult Satamanyu about this, a guy in overalls said, the sort of handsome one, no shirt, with a regular old kerchief around his neck, not tie-dyed.

42

You might think that the beginning of a completely new saga. You might flash-forward to those guys bringing the awkward problem of our non-compliance to their guru, being told in short order simply to abduct us, that we'd be very glad in the future to have submitted to our fate as aiders and abettors of this crucial journey. That we would, in fact, thank them for virtually hog-tying us, throwing us into the bowels of that boat as they wheeled it out of the garage, down that *suburbo* street, over to Muir Beach, where they intended to launch the whole affair in a week or two. That we'd be overjoyed they had issued us aprons at last.

None of this happened. After a while, the music went on again, this time Judy Collins singing about someone's perfect body for the hundredth time. The reefer circle started to circle up once more, those guys on their way to being wasted again. There was an argument going on about Nietzsche and Marshall McLuhan in one corner as someone on the other side of the room was thinking back, past how many lives to his very first one, to that spirit he still felt alive in him, a little child about 100 BC—boy or girl, it wasn't clear—in Persia, modern-day Iran. He was ticking off the sights there. A lot of boats seemed to be made out of paper. He saw a pier, definitely made out of gold. Those listening, a couple of them, bent forward, amazed.

Frances still wanted to know things about Ned. This *Lives of the Saints* approach was okay for a while; it sort of pumped her up, but she wanted the real scoop. She got Mukunda out on the porch and I could see they were head to head, locked in talk. I was wondering where they would put us for the night when one of the robes silently appeared at my side with a pile of blankets and two pillows, and showed me to a tiny back room near the bathroom.

You two can sleep here, he said. This is where Satamanyu stays when he's in town.

I thought he lived around here.

No, he's in Santa Rosa, the robe said. Not that far away but yeah, he needs a place to crash when he comes and stays late. That cat's so fucking old, he said, bowing his head with great piety.

I felt pretty old myself, thoroughly exhausted, starting to get that hollow feeling under my ribs, always a sign.

Will you tell Frances this is where we'll be? That I brought her stuff in here?

He would, he promised. And I was closing my eyes, knowing Ned had probably slept there too, between putting them straight on Bertrand Russell and telling them how to fly. I could see him, that beautiful, rapt face in Kevin's photograph, floating there in its deep quiet. Two minutes and then, who knows how long. I was out of it, completely.

43

We were saying good-bye the next morning, right near the plum tree Ned had woven up and made sacred. It looked perfectly normal. Leaves. Nice long branches. And caught in the act of blossoming though had it lived in Illinois, we'd be waiting a month for that burst of color. Here, maybe it was flowering its heart out all the time in that non-stop sunlight. It was confusing. It was also Wednesday. We were headed south, to Big Sur.

Like what always seemed to happen when we left anywhere, we were loaded down with food. Only these guys gave us old cottage cheese containers of the lentil-rice stuff and two spoons. More of that heavy bread—which made me wonder why they were scrounging around for a cook in the first place. They clearly had a treasure among them already. They gave us fruit too—some beyond imagining: starfruit with its lime-green tart sweetness, a mango with its leathery skin. Shashee himself was driving into San Francisco; he'd give us a lift. *SF,* he called it—so *that* was an option—and he would be going as far as Pacifica but we'd be on Highway 1 by that time, so could just keep on—as he said—keeping on, in that direction.

En route, we heard Shashee's life story: his Seventh-day Adventist childhood in Kansas City, his flipping out on drugs at the Be-In almost four years ago in Golden Gate Park, his finding his way up toward Santa Rosa, his meeting Satamanyu who saved his life and blew his mind, and now this boat thing, this Peru-or-bust thing. He was still furious at the Diggers at that Be-In—the so-called *Gathering of the Tribes*—handing LSD out to people willy-nilly, along with turkey sandwiches.

It's not the acid so much, he said, but the turkey. Can you picture that? Urging someone to eat meat? What full-tilt jerks!

And then Frances and I heard about other outrageous carnivores in his past. Once, visiting in Oakland, he opened the fridge. And I thought he was my friend, Shashee was saying, until I saw that big chicken leg there on a plate.

He couldn't get over it. Chicken! Do you believe that? he asked twice as he pulled the car over to drop us off. It seemed bigger than one life, almost a rhetorical question. I tried to look sufficiently alarmed.

We stood for a bit on the ramp near Daly City. A guy in two long braids driving a station wagon stopped, the front seat piled high with old newspapers.

You two can get in back, he said through the open window. But don't expect me to talk much. I'm thinking way too hard about too many things.

Okay with us, I wanted to say though that seemed rude.

Only, where you headed? he asked.

Big Sur, Frances said.

I'll drop you there. And don't get me wrong. It's fine if you babes talk to each other. But you have to swear: not one word to me.

44

So we took him at his word—no words—and acted like he was our personal chauffeur, like we'd be calling out *home, James!* any second. I mean to say we totally ignored him as he glumly drove on, down the most breathtaking highway, maybe in the world. Pretty soon, once we were out of the city, it was one sheer drop to the sea. And we were looking out and over, right into all that lash and wave.

We sank back in our seats, nearly blotto at the beauty out there. Riveted, I guess, drunk with it or at least stunned. This was the California of postcards and dreams, of Robinson Jeffers, Gary Snyder, John Muir. And of all the druggies come west, I suppose, at least the exuberant sort who opened outward, not fixed the whole time on their troubles and their bad trips. But I was nosy and earthbound, still wondering about Mill Valley and what Frances might have turned up at the end as I was falling asleep in that back room, sharing the space with Satamanyu's old guy spirit no doubt puttering around near the ceiling, his astral home turf.

So what's the biz on Ned? I said, after the first wash of amazement had receded a little and we were beginning to take our luck for granted, the astonishing chance to see all this.

I knew you'd ask, Frances said, and—what's it been? About ten hours since I talked to that guy, counting the time we were sleeping? Hey, you held off! Not bad.

Fair enough, I said. I know it's none of my business.

Frances wasn't finished staring out the window. She stayed glued there, glancing at me now and then.

That's okay, she said. To tell the truth, what's-his-face—Mukunda—wasn't all that forthcoming. Maybe that's part of what those drugs do to you, zap your memory or something. I don't know.

She stopped for a moment, still looking toward the ocean. I wasn't sure if I was supposed to say anything or not.

Like, I heard that stuff again. You know, how smart Ned was and everything. There's some talk of writing this down, the things he said. I guess one of them might do it. Sort of a mantra around there anyway, right? You could just pick those bits out of the air: Ned this, Ned that, far out far out far out. . . .

That tree business, I said.

Yeah, and the learn-to-fly story. And the ways to get high just looking at something close, for a long time. Even some stupid twig. Even your own hand.

Frances, they love Ned there. That's a great thing, isn't it?

Sure. I know. But Mukunda was worried too. He finally coughed that up. He tried to put the best light on it: *Frances,* he goes, *Ned stepped into inner space and didn't want to come back.* I guess one translation would be drugs and more drugs until who knows what. Until Ned was scaring himself, I guess. That's what I think.

Could you get to a place there was no self left to scare? The thought itself was scaring me. But maybe that was the point.

Our driver, in the left lane now, abruptly swerved right, mumbling something we couldn't make out. And the car just behind us roared ahead. Frances sank back in her seat.

But it was more than that, you know? Ned was always so damn curious. About everything. And innocent mainly. Like, that's what Mukunda probably meant too. But those guys got freaked out, just watching him after a while. And get this bizarre little fact: he said Ned started to glow in the dark. Is that bullshit or what?

Bet even their guru can't do that, I said.

They almost called the hospital too, when he climbed up on the roof and wouldn't come down for four days.

That spun me right off—Ned up on the roof of that house, starry night after starry night, his long tangle of red hair fanned out, some kind of weird halo effect. Like those ancient saints in the desert, the pole-sitters, up high for months, years of visions. And that thing about flying. What really struck me was that I once dreamt someone telling me exactly what Ned had told those guys, that it's all in the small of the back. And easy. Just lie down and lift off, like this, like this. What a breathtaking simple idea. And Ned. What had he found up there on that roof, what was the difference to him between waking and sleeping? Maybe nothing at all, the whole notion of time bluing out in some slow dissolve, mimicking what the sky does most summer afternoons.

I guess Ned *was* fucked up, Frances said finally. A little. Not as bad as Kevin seems to think though.

I could see her tense up. Just the word *Kevin* did it to her, just her saying it out loud.

It's beautiful here, isn't it? she said, the ocean and all?

Yeah, I said. And if someone told me about this place—I'd never believe them in a million years.

We both looked out the window then, past Santa Cruz and Monterey now and pretty much the rest of the way, joining our driver with all his things to think about.

45

The ways one could be fucked up and still semi-function seem so multiple and strange. You can watch that happen, to others and to yourself; this is what it's like to get older. It's possible to think forward *and* back like Janus, that Roman god of doorways or maybe more like those stupid bobble heads going every which way that people used to put in the back window of their cars. That's the good part, looking here, then there—even forward and back to Netherwood Co-op again, Mr. Ts'ou tucked in among us, that guy from the other side of the planet. He did talk about things besides ducks at the edge of that lake in Madison, besides the lofty/funny renaming always ongoing in that house. But things darken fast. You never know when it might happen. One day we came back to find Mr. Ts'ou boarding up his windows, his the only bedroom on the first floor of the place. He was nailing in great sheets of plywood.

Mr. Ts'ou, what's going on?

He wouldn't respond directly. He only wondered if we'd seen any Chinese people lately, three men to be exact, coming into the house and asking what it was like to be a member of the co-op, who lived here, how much it cost.

We nosed around on that one. And yes, Callahan had met those guys, and Kiva, Liz too. They had dropped by, full of questions about the place. Liz described their gray trench coats like something out of a bad detective film, how they had leaned forward, only semi-listening to the lowdown on Netherwood, their faces hard to read. They kept looking around. Their English wasn't all that good.

Mr. Ts'ou nodded gravely. We must keep the door locked, he said. It is important.

It's the goon squad, Kiva insisted later, it must be. I bet they're Chinese government spies checking up on Joe, no kidding. This is creeping me out. Maybe they're out to claim him back. Something bad's coming down. I feel it, man. They're going to snatch him away in the dead of night.

Or not, said Mika. Get a grip. Those guys probably just need a place to live, that's all. Listen, even Joe has a trench coat. You're going to make a big deal out of that? Come on. I think Joe's paranoid. You know, a stranger in a strange land? He's getting weird on us. Don't you get weird too.

Hey, it's always a strange land in America, Kiva said.

Either way, it was Mr. Ts'ou then, spending hours in his physics lab, showing up only at supper, mostly worried-unto-furtive, making sure both doors locked behind him—the main entrance to the house as well as his own room, pitch black at all hours now, given those sheets of plywood tacked up. Maybe he was safer, but no light lived there.

Danger takes on all forms, inside, outside, real, and imagined; one can get huge or shrink to nothing under it. Or simply coexist there, sending out one lame and passionate S-O-S after another to the likes of St. Anthony, that he find something more abstract and important than keys or car rides this time—peace of mind, for instance. *All will be well* may be a useful mantra too as you fall asleep at night or any old *Hail Mary* hanging on from childhood, rushed through in whatever lapsed way. *The holy rumble,* a nun once told us in grade school; that's what it took to keep the earth spinning, what the contemplative Orders still send up at Matins, Lauds, Compline, all various points between, those ancient marked hours of day and night. That holy rumble: what Buddhists chant for years on end.

But here was Ned, another dark flash of him. Ned, up on that roof alone, those Mill Valley guys circling below wondering what to do now, to call the hospital or not, how even to think what he might be thinking.

46

So we got to Big Sur. I don't know what the place is like now but then, there wasn't all that much, in the way of stores and streets and houses, I mean. The ocean, of course, its immense heart beating as usual, those mountains beginning just a shade east of the highway and rearing into cliffs or sometimes they gently rose. No town, not even a village, but maybe there was such a thing sitting on the edge of the sea all along. I just can't remember. The Esalen Institute had been built much earlier on that particular and desolate stretch of coast. The guy with the braids pulled the car over where the highway ribboned out not too far from that place. It was a little way south, he told us, its various buildings and baths spread out below, near the water. Above, we saw a house and so many trees, a long, wide stretch of grass and weeds and wildflowers.

Later girls, our driver said. It'll have to be in some other realm though, he added a little sadly as we stepped from the station wagon. He sped off, not even looking back in the rearview mirror. Frances pointed up, toward the house.

Emil White's place, she said. Right there.

It was the first I'd heard that name. We hoisted our packs and started up the pitted-out skinny road of gravel and dirt, turning slightly when it turned to meadow surrounded by a grove of giant redwoods. We saw nothing much really until we were directly facing the house and there they were, two young women on the grass, eyes shut, lying out in a thin channel of sun without clothes, in the buff, *au naturel.* And motionless, like they had frozen there in that narrow flashflood of daylight.

Frances, I said, keeping my voice down, what's *this* all about? She probably waved the question off or made some crack about girls just needing their vitamin D bath. But I don't remember that either.

47

Certain moments open and you fall right in, sucked back to some previous elsewhere. Still, this was 1971; this was California, the ocean seizing up and letting go behind us, a casualness expected before all things sacred or profane, or sacred *and* profane—so went the deepest intuition: *both, at once.* And now these two young women, so close to us in age, basking in their all-together in that sea-air light, apparently not a second thought about it.

And me—I was rich in second thoughts, only three years out of that Catholic all-girl high school, St. Patrick's Academy. But it wasn't what one might think, the world of that place—or even the thoughts—most of us caught up in a particularly funny, ironic, self-deprecating method of understanding most matters. Including the fact of our bodies. *Yes,* our resident comic genius Deborah Durbin liked to sing out with a sweet sting to her voice: *yes, your body is a temple, girls, and boys will love to worship there.* Of course, not one of us—with the exception perhaps of Crazy Alex—had any experience of such worldly liturgy.

The nuns were certain though. They were sure of our dates, that we were going out each weekend, heavy-breathing the only soundtrack. Sister Sulpice especially, one of the ancient ones who turned yellow in winter, who taught me French with almost no success, was diligent in her mission to give us tips, to keep us clear about the appropriate thing to do on these supposed dates. We looked forward to her class, if only for the next installment on how to behave, to dress, what to take with us on those occasions—*just in case*—though we had full-fledged doubts there'd ever be any use for the information. What *was* the chance? No boys in that school, after all. Every spring it was Mr. Evans, our old soft-spoken janitor, who was honored in the school annual as *man of the year,* his picture there, smiling over the broom he held jauntily, at an angle. No contest in that contest.

But those dating tips. I've told them countless times, to groups of friends, large and small, who have passed them on to others, even worked them into their own fiction. They're like the St. Anthony prayer, I suppose; they bear repeating. Certain ones shine, stay put in the mind to haunt there, to cast their shadows. You could start with the most predictable—*don't wear pearls, they reflect down* or *don't eat at places with white tablecloths, boys will think of bedsheets,* or *never never order ravioli, they remind boys of pillows.* Great dictums, all worth reciting again. There were others that stopped our hearts, made us each choke in delight silently, straight-faced as we'd trained ourselves to be, dying for the bell so we could sprint to the lavatory and laugh ourselves sick. But one was a treasure of invention, immediately our favorite of all, one we constantly retold until it worked—I see this now—as Bach worked his fugues, intricately connected, a model of symmetry and strangeness.

It was fairly elaborate, even for Sister Sulpice's gothic imagination. There was set design involved in this particular dating tip, high theater. And special effects. It had to be raining, number one. There were costumes as well. Surely you'd be wearing a skirt on such a date. And the cast, a Cecil B. DeMille number—not one boy and a car but several people, way too many for the back seat especially. This was before seatbelts of course, a fact that allowed for certain party games like: how many bodies could you stuff in a car and still drive it? But yes, the dating tip in question—rainy day, check; you're in a skirt, check; maybe you'd be sitting jammed up in the backseat, double check. There were props too, crucial ones.

So, girls, Sister Sulpice said, you must must *must* carry with you a bag of little stones on such evenings. And the Chicago phonebook.

We looked puzzled.

Because, she said delicately, you see. . . . She cleared her throat before going on. Girls, remember please that the rain has probably been coming down since late afternoon. So—when you cross over each puddle, you need to remove your stones one by one and drop them *into* that water. She paused here; we leaned forward. *To break the reflection, girls,* she finally said with regret and resolve, *as quick as you can.*

I love the thought of her telling us this. I love especially the look on Deborah Durbin's face, fast turning purple as those words sank in, Durbin even now plotting the exaggerated version she would act out for us later next to the lavatory's steamy radiator or back behind the school near the Stations of the Cross as we waited for the bus to appear that afternoon. She would do all the pauses, make the same horrified expression, drop one by one each of those stones, a deft mime and maneuver.

And girls, said Sister Sulpice, about that phone book. If, and certainly I hope you *never* have to do this. . . . She stopped then for a second as though it might be too painful to go on. But *if,* she said, you *have* to sit on a boy's lap because there is so little room in that car, then you *must* put the Chicago phone book—at that time, at least three inches thick—*on the lap* before you sit down. You *do* understand, girls, don't you? Of course she never explained why this was advisable or necessary. We had to draw our own conclusions, and richly, most powerfully managed that. Which is, I have to admit, a strong argument for reserve, for a remote sensing approach to erotica.

Nevertheless—again—this was now, this was California. And Sister Sulpice in those intervening three years might have yellowed up beyond hope, come apart, shards of her slipping into the next life.

In fact, we passed the two sunbathers without further notice. They never opened their eyes or moved in the slightest. In a flash, we were at the house, ushered in warmly by Emil White, who was asking us questions, offering lunch. Not a word was said about those young women. I looked out his side window a few minutes later. They were gone.

48

House or cabin or camp. Beyond that, how to describe such a rugged, glorious place. I think of it as isolated, a spot where one looked down and out and over, that we walked a long way to find it, a set of small switchbacks all the way up from Highway 1. Maybe it had a big bay window, the house itself in a kind of T-shape and at least five rooms. Or maybe none of these things. After all, memory is a box. Things stored there so carefully can disappear, just like that. Where do they go? And what is the future without them? I suppose Ned would have said it's all present tense when you come right down to it. That's what we really are.

I only mean whatever its accuracy, it's entirely real. I think we did pass a mailbox with *Emil* carved into it, that there was a kind of porch, an open deck up a few steps from which you could see that *sea* raging out and pulling back. I could be hallucinating. *Retrospect* can do that. I know I learned the names and timing of things later, that these were called the Santa Lucia Mountains, rising up immediately east of that thin wire, Highway 1, itself up from the ocean; that Emil White had built his house on the edge of Graves Canyon; that he came to it late—in 1965—after many years living at Big Sur in other locations, up on Partington Ridge and above Anderson Creek, even down at the Esalen Institute, where he was officially the caretaker for a while.

But for all I knew at first glance—given his comfort, how sweetly lived-in everything looked—he'd spent practically a lifetime in that house. What did I know about anything? The old questions I should have been asking Frances, I never bothered or even thought to. How in the world did Emil meet Ned, that singular haunted and brilliant kid from Illinois? How did Frances seem to know Emil so well? These appeared to be givens, things answered with a simple *because,* all of it cast into the no-question-about-it present moment, all *is is is,* no *was* and its accompanying reasons in the mix. But why did the guy act like he knew me?

We still had the food from Mill Valley, the two cottage cheese containers of lentils and rice, that serious bread. So we made a counteroffer to his offer to lay out a decent lunch.

Ah, you two beautiful women have brought me beautiful bread! Emil said. And a biblical stew one would sell a birthright for. Yes, yes, add it to our table! Then he was slowly peeling and separating oranges, cutting a block of cheese into the thinnest slices, looking up at us in such an endearing way, like it was the most lovely task of all, this drinking us in.

Oh Emil, Frances said in a brand-new voice.

He was nothing if not gracious. I wasn't used to this. It seemed over the top and stagy. At best, corny. At worst, on the lechey side. In any case dated, set back in time, those soulful looks of his, and not a little unnerving. *Beautiful women?* Come on. But I could see he meant it fondly. Or perhaps he was storing up for later, point blank and unashamedly coming on to us, to both of us, just in case. I mean, there *were* two girls outside moments ago, sunning every inch of themselves. It seemed impossible to me, given his age, but clearly he was some kind of chick magnet.

The accent was slight—not German, I learned, but Austrian. He'd been born in 1901 in Galicia, a part of Poland or the Ukraine, depending, though when he was very little, his family fled first to a small town just inside Austria and then to Vienna, then he, alone, at 16, to Budapest, where he had about ten terrifying seconds facing a firing squad before he managed somehow to bolt and get away.

You see, they thought I was a Socialist, he told us. Oh no no, I wasn't anything at all—just out of there fast! I just wanted something to eat, I was starving!

Many unlikely adventures followed; he finally ended up in Chicago in the early '20s—his early 20s too—working at a bookstore. Via New York first, Paris before that, Switzerland before that. Oh, and so much went on after! Too much to tell. Alaska! The Yukon! he told us. Then this place, Big Sur. Ahhh! he half-sighed, half-said. A paradise! I am so happy.

How could we not nod and agree?

But your trip! he said like he'd known us all our lives and we'd finally returned to his open arms.

If I could have time-traveled years ahead, I would have thought of my old, beloved cousin Elinor Brogden then, her favorite joke in her 80s when I spoke to her by phone, her wanting us to drive up to *old Madison-Wis,* as she called it, and visit: *all is forgiven, please come home!* And later, when she was really failing: *Reports of my death are greatly exaggerated!* she told me, gleefully quoting Mark Twain.

Does that mean your bad habits are still intact? I asked.

Yes, she said, bring up the gin! And don't forget the piggy chews!—her code for chips, dip, all manner of fancy delectable treats. But it was Emil's next line too, I would have heard Elinor singing that out, perfect: *My dears, my dears, my dears, he was saying, tell me everything so far!*

That was lunch. I did the math. Emil White was 70 years old. A small shock. This ordinary guy, wiry, on the short side, almost elfin and pretty long in the tooth now in spite of his full head of wavy hair: he was downright luminous. And why is it, I think now, that the old—wild, wry Elinor, and Emil too—appeared so unburdened, released somehow and open to the world while the young carried what seemed years behind them, the dense and troubling weight of a lifetime hardly begun?

I'm listening, Emil said. I want to hear it all!

49

In fact, I have only a vague idea what we told him of our trip. We no doubt talked through the basics—when and where we started, about Woody, a free man, sprung from the army at last, about those loser Lincoln boys in their wannabe hippie van, their cockeyed exuberance all the way west. Blah blah, this and that. I know we mentioned Mill Valley, the hare-brained perfectly earnest Peruvian boat-and-guru notion, the love story waiting to happen way below its astral plane. A treasure, I knew even then. A perfect cameo of that crazy era. But they were all perfect cameos, each the real thing, which is why they were destined to be near clichés of that time. It couldn't be helped. The pure forms of things, how they can both *mean* and *be* beyond themselves over and over. What has William Gass said? Clichés are the only friends we really know. I figure they're practically tribal wisdom, the way knowledge is passed seemingly without any effort at all.

But in the story of our story, I noticed Frances completely skipped the painful parts, about Joyce and Kevin for instance. And Ned. I remember that: not a word about Ned *before* the crash though presumably Emil knew things.

Our host was clearing the dishes now, taking them over to the sink in his small kitchen, refusing any help from us. And as he worked, he talked. He had a theory. We were tied to the great cycles of the earth: rain and then sun, night then day. We must live with the sweet weight of that. Take and do and do *for,* and return things to their place. He said he liked the idea of preparing simple food, eating well and slowly, then washing the plates, rinsing them, putting them on the rack to dry. A symmetry to it. A kind of harmony. Mindfulness, he said.

Thus Emil—so much from another time—was a cameo of that moment-in-time too. Normally, I would have given Frances the hairy eyeball at his soliloquy, the move a throwback to high school when we called such a remark *a granny tip.* We'd look serious enough while someone spewed out the most sanctimonious dribble. *Thanks granny!* we'd say finally, laughing too hard. But I could tell: Emil meant every word. All seemed new, the way he said it, one grand and complicated thought with many parts. So I behaved myself: no hairy eyeball, no wise-ass comment.

Ah, but I have another plan now, he said. You are my beautiful guests. He halfway bowed. What *was* this thing with bowing? I will take you to Esalen!

Even before our ride here and the guy with the braids mentioning it, I had heard of the Esalen Institute—probably from *Newsweek* or *Life* magazine. Esalen, epicenter of hip weirdness, group massage, and gestalt and encounter groups, *oming* out the wazoo. I imagined people on a sunny deck over waves crashing below, young and old doing their yoga equally, slow-moving contortions with deliberate names: the downward-dog, the welcome-sunbeam, the upside-down-inside-out-flower, whatever. I don't know. Everyone finding himself, finding herself, though in my case, I wasn't sure what I'd do with such a self—who knows how many selves—turning up from some long lost place. And *who* are *you*? the famously arch bong-sucking caterpillar asked Alice in her Wonderland.

Oh yeah, said Frances, wow, Esalen. We would totally dig that, Emil.

50

We set out. That sounds like the opening of some great epic: *we set out.* But we did. Because Esalen wasn't far, first the easy stretch down to the highway, passing the meadow, those serious redwoods and the friendship of their shade. As we walked south, we listened to Emil playing docent, telling us Esalen's convoluted history which seemed to spring from, well, from a real-live springs—Slate's Hot Springs because the Slates had homesteaded the place in 1883, to be exact. And some people still called it that even though a family called Little had had it for a while.

Then Murphy's Hot Springs, Emil said, when it changed hands in 1914—Dr. Henry Murphy, with a kind of hospital down there. Before that, long ago, the Esselen Indians soaked in those waters. And for decades it really was the only place in Big Sur to get a decent bath, before plumbing and electricity hit, certainly before Highway 1 was eked out of the rock face by convict labor in the '30s. But those Indians—that's how Esalen got its name. Because a second Murphy—Henry's son, Michael—named it that on the advice of another longtime Big Sur resident, one Harry Ross. And this particular Murphy ran it now.

Who has big big ideas, Emil added with a wink.

That wink thing seemed dated too, and corny, like we'd been let in on something we knew zero about before. It was embarrassing and flattering—two things that often go together.

We walked along, Emil pointing out the distant gulls, the buzzards as bits of wheeling black, then his favorites, the pelicans and red-tailed hawks, and trees—Monterey pines up the mountain, the bay laurels. We could smell eucalyptus too, emphatic and spicy, otherworldly. The wildflowers were starting up everywhere, near sweeps of them: the red poppy, the blue lupine, the tiny yellow buttercup. Oh, so beautiful! Emil said. And in the ocean, we might get lucky and see whales since it was March. Their spouts, their blowing their tops way out there. He told us about things we wouldn't see: rare wild orchids, delicate, every shade of purple in those woods, and the Zen monastery established not long ago, Tassajara—I would learn about their famous bread book later—though one *could* hike into the mountains to find that place. Did we know that Elizabeth Taylor and Richard Burton filmed *The Sandpiper* here six years ago? What a movie! Now *there's* a magnificent woman, Emil said, stopping in his tracks, eyes lifted toward heaven. He sighed a long, appreciative theatrical sigh.

We were nearing the place. *Esalen Institute, by Reservation Only,* the wooden sign read.

Think nothing of *that,* Emil said, dismissing it with a wave of his hand.

51

I'll try to describe Esalen though I recall so little that I feel like a blind person—how I imagine that must be like—getting the room by feel, the woods or meadow by scent, the winds that bring that scent, a shift in that wind, sometimes cooler, sometimes warmer. The sound of birds there, the chickadee, the thrush, and vireo beyond melodic into utter transformation which must add depth, foreground and background, a long, lonely widening out, this trying to remember: *here, where-I-am* and *there, where-everything-else-on-the-planet-must-be.*

But it wasn't that exactly. I can't make any romantic claims in spite of the sea, the wash of the breakers on the rocks below, the immediate no-doubt-about-it raw beauty of the place. You need a jaded eye; you hope for that, like when watching for an eclipse in full squinting daylight, you're told to wear special dark glasses, or just not look directly. Anything to protect yourself, to find a sane way to witness.

We tagged along after Emil White, who, as honorary mayor of Big Sur—so he called himself—apparently knew every last person there, those in serious conversation, their heads close; those sitting alone, seeming happy enough to stare out to sea, having downed some sort of psychedelic minutes, hours ago—or perhaps not; those on the big deck doing yoga or Tai Chi, just as

I had pictured they'd be doing; those down to wearing almost nothing, in what might have passed as a bathing suit or the few in truly nothing, stretched out on the wide benches, sunning every possible spot as the girls in Emil's yard had, eyes closed as theirs had been, trusting the world to be indifferent about them. And even though that world might be looking hard, in praise or in judgment or with ill-intent held barely at bay, they were free, *past all that.* They didn't need to look back.

We walked around the place. Emil would turn, remembering we were there and happily introduce us. I tried to disappear at such moments—and maybe Frances too—both of us smiling and nodding, my hoping, in any case, that this sticky gleam of attention would pass quickly. As for how we all *looked,* thus how Frances and I were locked in and scrutinized in the larger frame of the place, that was more complex. Off the common parlance of *casual* or more than casual, our *scruffy*—and, by this time, our semi-*unwashed*—might have jumped a line: jeans that didn't bell-bottom enough at the ankle, my frayed T-shirt the wrongest navy blue against the bright, winged-out, striped, polka-dotted, paisley, fringed, drapey, beaded, flowing, or tight-fitting get-ups people wore. And just because I had loaded all my bras in a cardboard box in a surge of melodramatic free thinking, mailing them home my first semester of college—that hardly qualified me for Esalen.

More importantly, we were pretty vague about *Fritz*—Fritz Perls—and *Abe*—Abraham Maslow and who knows who else, the official demigods in that fiefdom whose code phrase was "human potential." So their jargon talk-talk just hung there, an airy thought-bubble around us. The best I could do for the moment was a little Alan Watts and R. D. Laing with a side of William Blake, who only occasionally, however urgently, made sense to me. But I still have a glorious half second of that, my walking home from class in Champaign the previous fall, puzzling out a passage of his, let loose in the bluest air. Then something flashed high above me.

How do you know but ev'ry Bird that cuts the airy way,
Is an Immense world of delight, clos'd by your senses five?

52

Whatever Blake might have thought of that lovely instant of release, his words into real time and flight, the completely alive and equal feel of that, the thing is—the great world sometimes goes quite another way. Sometimes its weight is too daunting to measure, its duration sudden and dark.

Earlier, for instance, that spring of the trip, I had this bright idea: to learn about Africa. With great excitement, I signed up for a course—West African History—and showed up at the first meeting in January, oddly *not* in a regular classroom or lecture hall. In the professor's office, an elegant windowed space in an old building with creaky floors, the scent of wood oil and dust. Total enrollment: four, the other students male and older, much older, it seemed to me. I think now they were probably graduate students but I was too clueless even to grasp that shift in station.

We were given tea. There was an oriental rug on the floor. The professor wore a tweed sport coat with those classic elbow patches, as if putting on such a thing meant serious work with hammer and wedge, saw and file, that one such jacket would be enough for a decade of hard everyday use. He was—I'd guess now—in his late 50s, urbane and witty, languid in that offhand, clipped British sort of way. He'd lean back and laugh, and then return to the conversation, smoking a cigarette as if dream-struck for a moment. He obviously knew the other three members of the class; they bantered on about Senegal, how peanuts were up and fish was down, how the students were stirring in Dakar, demonstrations against Senghor quite possible again. And how far had each of us gotten in the past few months, in our study of Wolof? The professor landed on me first, with this question.

Wolof? I said. I'm sorry, I don't know what that is. Is that someone's name?

The main native language, one of the students whispered to me. Besides French, of course.

But the conversation was already elsewhere—to the other troubles Senegal's president, that Senghor, a poet apparently, was having—before I could say could say another word. A good thing, probably. I didn't even know it had been a French colony.

You've read Senghor's *Nocturnes,* no doubt? the professor asked one of us.

Oh yes, whoever-he-was answered brightly, a beautiful book! And our professor, pleased with that, took another exquisitely slow drag off his cigarette.

Yes, but tell me. Given recent history, are we to read such poetry ironically, do you think? Is that how we should begin? Or is Senghor absurdly naive? He looked around, locking us into this question.

All except me. I was thrashing about in deep water by now, way under sea level. I was locked nowhere, rather, locked out, into some blurry pre-nowhere. Nonetheless, it was a gift, a brief vision, I suppose, before I dropped the class that day, of a world

I'd need way more ammo to enter, its complications ongoing, full of intrigue and good carpets, questions and assertions, tea and imported cigarettes whose smoke climbed and turned in the steady afternoon light.

53

A glimpse then: such are the moments of perpetual beginning. To be stopped, to feel the starting point so keenly. That was Esalen too, by will or accident.

So you two are—from where?

Frances and I would mumble what we could to answer, obviously self-conscious and awkward—no doubt a problem more serious than how we dressed or what we'd read since that state of being is deeply contagious; its stain can spread. Meeting strangers, especially older ones—and everyone seemed older at Big Sur, well-spoken, earnest, at ease—I mostly lived uncomfortably in such a state, a kind of suffocating thought-bubble that lasted well into my 30s. Even now in any gathering, large or small, I can blink back to that mode, fully unnerved, time slowing to the awful tick tick of a clock in the empty room of my head. The fact is, it's crucial not to give a rat's ass about what happens, or why, so that the *you* in there shrinks down. Then all improves dramatically. Then you find words and thoughts. Or they find you. But I was years away from this most useful delusion. We—Frances and I—were basically mute.

I'm using the royal *we* here. I take it back. It's not altogether fair because about Frances I was never so sure. But I have an analogy, a sideways way to describe her, to lock her into semi-focus.

It was one of Ned's images, one he must have clipped from *Life* magazine for his collage back at the Sunderland's, Robert Frost at Kennedy's inauguration, a thing my family had witnessed—in a manner of speaking. We were Democrats, and as Catholics much excited by this impossible turn of events. I was nine, the television on; we were watching with my grandmother, born not too long after Frost, in 1883. But that raw and blistering cold inaugural day in Washington, the poet slowly climbed the steps to the tall outdoor podium they'd made for the young president's swearing in, and began to recite, his famously full head of white hair taken this way and that by the wind. It was 1961. My 77-year-old grandmother leaned forward, squinting at the TV.

That old man, she said with fierce disapproval, that old man should have a hat on!

Nanny, that's Robert Frost! we cried.

I don't care who it is, she told any and all of us.

Which is only to say that Frances struck me, at times, as my no-nonsense grandmother had, largely unimpressed by the exalted. Because no doubt Frances would have taken in stride that talk of Senegal and Senghor too, finding a way to hold herself together in that terrifying, book-lined office. Mostly, she went about her business seemingly unbothered, born to any turn of events.

That included only half-listening now as Emil set about being the good docent again, telling us about the Lodge where people ate, the massive eucalyptus tree planted by that earlier owner, Tom Slate, at the end of the nineteenth century, showing us the string of little cabins where sometimes Joan Baez lived for weeks at a time. He mentioned that Aldous Huxley showed up briefly once, and Hunter Thompson and Ginsberg and Kerouac maybe more than once. And that the oldest building was a family home called the Big House, right on the beach. I kept waiting for Emil to say something about Ned coming to Esalen. I mean, I could place him in any of these spots, staring straight into the sun even, for dangerous minutes at a time. Then doing the encounter thing out of curiosity or hope, or the scream therapy, the group massage, the blind-folded walk.

Emil! Frances said as expectant as a kid, like come on, you *promised*. So where are the baths?

Emil's eyebrows went up. He smiled at us. Yes, yes, he said, pointing vaguely down and up and out to sea. Three directions at once.

54

I think, in fact, the baths *were* via some steps, an open then wooded and wandering narrow path, stone steps cut right into the rock wall to the ocean. I almost seem to recall that. Or rickety stairs, rather life-threatening stairs, but again, who knows? Emil told us that old porcelain bathtubs had been improbably brought—by ship—and set up there shortly after the Civil War, then the more impressive claw-footed, cartoon-like kind in 1914, ordered by Dr. Murphy and arriving the same way over the sea for the blasts of hot mineral water piped out of the cliffside stained and layered by its chemicals to rich grays and whites, off-reds and blues. I've seen wonderful photographs with the likes of Henry Miller amused, poised over those tubs in the '50s. The banned and celebrated writer Henry Miller—Emil White's great friend and longtime hero, the one for whom Emil opened and answered mail, years and years of it, and carried groceries, did general cabin repair, for whom he was champion and confidant and guardian angel. Miller, to whom Emil would eventually, even before his own death, dedicate his house as memorial, *The Henry Miller Library*, open to all comers now, there on Highway 1. But I learned about their extraordinary friendship later. Emil didn't say much to us then—nothing really—about his famous pal.

What I directly recall about the Esalen baths was this: big stone troughs built of concrete cinder blocks that might seat a small gaggle of people. Open-air, sort of, with a roof and a platform hanging in a precarious way about a hundred feet above the ocean crashing below, its flashing kelp and foam. The deck, balcony, patio—whatever you want to call it—was appointed with wide tables, the kind sunbathers lie out on, the kind my great aunt Maud used when my grandmother—the one so irritated with Frost—needed a whack, a work-over, an "adjustment"— Aunt Maud, who claimed to be the first female graduate of the College of Osteopathic Medicine in Kirksville, Missouri, 1912 or so. Those afternoons in the '50s, early '60s, we'd walk over to Maud's house on Scott Street and I'd watch my grandmother hoist herself up on just such a table. That was downstate, Tuscola, Illinois, where my mother's family—the Taylors—had already put in at least two generations of hardscrabble farming.

Here at Big Sur, beyond those tables, the sulfur water in the baths so stinging hot it was *let's wait for a bit while this sucker cools down.* After a while you'd ease yourself in, inch by inch, instantly lobster-red, all the blurry parts under water, getting used to it anyway. I didn't want to think about that proverbial frog slowly lulled to a quick unhappy end in his gradually brought-to-a-boil kettle. Besides, that analogy didn't hold, the basic principle working in a way I couldn't quite figure.

Those famous baths: the place I both saw and read about later. The fact is—the play of light was unstoppable. I was squinting even in my bad sunglasses. It was steamy, a number of naked people running about. Not running. More, they were sunk to their pleasure in the hottest water imaginable. Or they lay out quietly on the Aunt Maud tables in the sun. Some just sat on the edge of those troughs probably waiting for the water to cool down, not a stitch on, chatting like it was a church basement somewhere, the Altar and Rosary Society or the Knights of Columbus about to start up a monthly meeting.

I said before: earnest, offhand, unembarrassed. Trademark Esalen. I would have made a wry remark to Frances but I was too intimidated. Even now, in memory. Still, I recall looking around in vain for a face showing signs of mutiny, an edge of irony in some quizzical expression which to me always suggests something of interest stirring. But zip—*nada,* as Crazy Alex would say. Not *that* sort of life on the planet though surely there were doubters among them. Of that, I'm certain. It's the human condition after all, probably what keeps the human part going.

To be honest, these blips in my side-vision happened so fast. And Frances and I were—supposed to drop trou and jump into those vats? I tried that daring movie-to-be in my head but I couldn't get past the opening credits. Just the logistics of such an act, let alone the modesty factor that loomed and cast its shadow—I stood there blankly under that shadow, no idea how this movie would play out. Would we strip and jump in and be changed forever? A long-haired guy approached us, fully apologetic. Hard to believe someone was in charge but I suppose he was.

Sorry people, he said. He cocked his head left, held out his empty hands to us. Hey, Emil, he brightened up, how ya' doing, man? And Emil, on cue, began cheerfully to introduce us while we, as usual, hung back.

So sorry, the guy said again. I got to tell you: big day, I guess. See the crowd in here right now? I don't know how long 'til there's room.

No one had a watch to give us an estimate of the wait. There wasn't any clock on the wall. For that matter, there wasn't really a wall in the normal way of walls.

55

That business of the body, unveiling it with such low-key ceremony—or none at all—to a cast of, if not thousands, at least more than one: what to think about that, when one is 20? When *I* was 20, I guess I mean. Or any age, if the truth be told. My experience with this sort of thing was, as a friend of mine liked to say of any near-miss chances, slim and none.

The slimmest, in fact, was closer to none in grade school—late spring, the very end of third grade for me—behind the house, in a back corner of our yard. One of the many kids from across the street—Ricky Vacarello probably, a highly advanced fourth grader—suggested we all retire there after supper to *show what we had.* He meant we were to pull down our pants and note the varied view. But it turned out so quickly managed that I barely recall anything. Except, naturally, that we had *done that,* the circle of us squeezed in behind the bushes between two rusted trash cans. The scene floated now in my blurry past. A mortal sin, for sure.

My brother was older. You dumbbell, he said. That's a *venial* sin. It hardly counts.

Besides, he pointed out, we hadn't seen that much anyway. Not really. In any case, *he* didn't need to bring it up the following Thursday morning when we'd be hauled out of class at St. Eugene's and trotted over to church to queue up at the confessional booths, to ready ourselves for Mass and communion the following day, the First Friday in June when a clean slate would be required.

My problem was more about language than guilt. The many times I'd confessed my back-talk-to-parents, meanness-to-my-brother, my lying about whatever small thing, pouting about this or that hadn't prepared me for *bless me Father, for I have sinned, I pulled down my pants in front of others behind the garbage cans in my own back yard.* Such a description had no ring to it, no official sounding bland-enough summary aura. I needed a tidy box, a category. It wasn't yet anything one could drop simply into a list of small undoings and move blithely on. That mystery about language is the oldest, most puzzling I know of—how it makes the lived thing real or not real or only partly, be it written or spoken in that long, seemingly easy passage from one human to another.

Sitting in the pew, waiting my turn via a semi-dire sign from Sister Mary Michael the Archangel, her forefinger pointing directly then crooked back to usher me toward the confessional, I flushed hot then cold. How to find words for this terrible sin? "Impure action"—the standard follow-up to "impure thought"—didn't seem to cover it. That sounded way worse than it actually was. Mainly we giggled, half of us closing our eyes anyway.

How I happened abruptly on *nudist colony* is unclear to me even now. Maybe I'd seen some reference in *Life* magazine or on TV. But I'd heard that people took walks, read the paper on park benches, ate at picnic tables, played tennis—small events of a life passed through entirely naked in such a place, nothing earth-shaking about that. It would be a big deal to us, of course, kids out back among those galvanized cans, and not exactly what we were up to. Still, the phrase felt close enough.

Bless me, Father, for I have sinned, I began the usual way, pouring out my clutch of failures and what seemed a credible number for each transgression: the lies, the turns of disobedience or impatience or rage. And, as if it happened at least every other week, out came the *and I went to a nudist colony.* That phrase seemed hyphenated, practically one word the way I rushed through it then nearly gulped it back.

Nothing was said for at least thirty seconds. The old priest must have been weary of hearing about back talk and stealing dimes from the morning's gaggle of young penitents. *A nudist colony?* he said slow enough and with interest. He had decidedly come to.

Yes, Father.

I see, he said. And were your parents there?

I considered this as shrewdly as any Jesuit might. Those gears supposedly inside one's head, clicking away, spinning on and by way of their lovely juice, I could feel them doing that, coming up with an answer. What is meant by the word *there?* I reasoned. How big is *there?* I mean, my parents *were* in the house, just a few yards away, probably watching *Gunsmoke* on TV. If *there* is defined as yard *and* house, wouldn't that be the ticket? Couldn't I say yes?

Yes, I said. They were there.

I see, said Father Maguire. I see, he repeated at least once more. I could hear the kids queued up outside, their rustle and fidgeting. They'd be wondering what was taking so long.

You realize this is a very serious matter, he finally said. Now, listen to me carefully: no matter what, no matter who insists, you are *not* to go there any more. Do you understand that, my child?

Yes, Father.

All right then. For your penance, say three Our Fathers, six Hail Marys for purity, and five Glory-Bes that the Holy Ghost guide you. Go in peace, my child.

I tore out of the confessional, back to the pew, not feeling all that newly hatched clean the way the nuns claimed I would. Their pitch seemed right off television, like an ad for a new detergent, or for hand soap a gleaming pink, sparking random bolts of lightning as it sat innocently on the bathroom ledge. I never spoke of our backyard, short-order *nudist colony* to my mother either. That is, until she was nearly 80. I thought she'd think the story funny by then, long out of the old neighborhood, her living in Florida for years.

Oh no . . . god. . . .you didn't tell him that! she stuttered. No wonder Father Maguire always looked at me crosswise! Mortified, she was shaking her head.

Truth is overrated. Big mistake, telling her even then.

56

Truth then. Part of that is your own parlor game, I guess, putting the puzzle together, making form, a way to calm down the excitable parts that don't quite fit—first in your own head, or later, when you try to make it presentable or at least coherent, to pass it on to others. Not exactly a parlor game. Sometimes everything is at stake.

The truth about Ned? I was losing focus here. What did Emil White know about what happened to him, his hitchhiking down here after the disaster with Joyce and Kevin, however well—or half-well—they meant, pasting him up in that wall of famous faces? And again, how did Emil even know him to begin with? Big Sur and DeKalb, Illinois—again, I couldn't imagine more different spots in the universe. I hoped Frances was getting an earful. Because we were walking around Esalen again.

Nothing quite fit. But why did I care so much? In some troubling way, was I falling *toward* Ned—was that love? or some unsteady almost-love?—as Frances collected all those parts of him left behind so she could slowly pull *away*? If not love, then call it an obsession, plain and simple, this *wanting to know* about Ned. I had no business, of course, no claim to any of it. So I'd wander off alone, leaving them under a tree, just the two of them. That was only proper, because there was a second reason too. As welcoming as Emil was—basically an old beatnik guy, Frances and

I decided—there was a reserve about him, an old-world formality. It wouldn't occur to him to include me in such a personal conversation.

But were they talking about Ned? It was not the sort of thing I could know for sure. One can't *overhear* that easily. I'd need some wired-up, remote sensing device. The trip so far was one thing, us holed up at the Sunderlands discussing every rage and outrage that night, or dealing with the crazy-ass boat guys in Mill Valley and what they had claimed, or Frances's reporting on Mukunda's take as we rode down to Big Sur under explicit instructions *not* to utter a word to our sad preoccupied driver. Mainly the whole business was unspoken; we were in our separate heads, piecing Ned's story together. That was the real point of the trip, wasn't it? When we did talk, I was the official *listener,* but I could have been anyone for that job. It was a matter of place and timing, my *happening* to be there. Her world seemed complete without me, even though it had shattered. So much is private, much of it too strange and uncertain to tell anyway. And half of that nobody knows, not even the person who knows it.

Soon enough, Emil copped a ride for us back to his place from a guy headed north to San Francisco. Just a day trip, he said though it seemed late for such a venture. Have to check things out up there, he said then smiled and waved after he dropped us off, speeding away until his car was a dot. Or maybe until it was swallowed up by the curve of the highway. I can't remember.

Well, that was pleasant. But the things I have to show you! Emil said as we walked up the path once more to the house he had built, those giant solitary redwoods so companionable together, the first thing I saw.

57

Supper was number one on the list, and this time Frances and I had nothing to bring to the table. But Emil set us to work cutting up carrots and onions and garlic while he deftly removed various boney bits from the chicken. I stared at the wine he poured for me, aware that I was underage. But maybe not in California, I reasoned. Of course, grass was illegal everywhere but that fact never seemed damning in the least. And the drinking laws in Illinois—now that I thought about it—never stopped anyone I knew either. I had a sip. And another. Emil was doing a stir-fry thing; he was making rice too. White rice—he was that kind of guy.

He was talking about beauty, mainly female beauty, but with the wave of his hand, the redwoods outside were involved. And the mountains and this particular canyon, the birds, and the ocean. Certainly the ocean. *All is one, when your eyes have been opened*—the usual stuff. Back to women though. He had something he wanted us to see after supper. But we took our time eating.

Taste every bite! was Emil's advice. Hmmm, he pronounced with delight, looking at Frances and then at me, back and forth like we were an important part of this delicious moment.

It occurred to me the guy was lonely. And we would *do* for right now. How else to explain it? Soon we were cleaning up, watching

Emil wash every dish lovingly by hand and set each in the rack to dry. It was slow-motion, excruciating to observe. *Beautiful* excruciating, since that was the theme, the house standard let loose on all-things-Emil. For years I'd think back to this small radiant vignette, this 70-year-old washing plate by plate and cup by cup, setting them to dry. Before long it got intertwined in my head with those lines of W. S. Merwin's about a similar moment of pure contentment:

> . . . *mountains like a rack of dishes*
> *in a house I love. . . .*

Now, my dears, Emil announced when he'd finished, I'll be right back. And he vanished to another room.

You okay? Frances mouthed at me from the other side of the table.

58

Emil returned with a small cardboard box. It was brimming with photographs, older ones in black and white, some larger than others, a few mounted on thick dark poster board with stylized art-deco frou-frou in the corners or along the right and left margins. He set the box down between us, Frances on the couch, me on an old hassock. Emil pulled up a kitchen chair and beamed at us.

We were talking about beauty. I want to show her to you.

He started taking them out of the box, photographs of his former wife, he told us, who lived in Australia now, but oh, look what she looked like!

Frances and I stared into the pictures, seemingly from the '30s or '40s, vintage film-noir contrast close-ups of yes, a beautiful woman. Or a woman herself convinced from the get-go—or by the photographer's certainty—of the truth of that. Beauty with a capital B, the kind that shouts itself hoarse, is most definitely willed and weighs a whole lot. Just picking up those pictures, I knew they'd be heavy. It was high drama. *Come with me—to the Casbah,* her hooded look seem to say, boring into anyone who happened by. *Bedroom eyes,* my mother and her friends would have called them. And my old cousin Elinor would have agreed too but *my, my, how gorgeous!* she would have said with genuine relish—and pleased our host, no end.

Emil's former wife had her head turned slightly in most of the photographs, half revealing, half concealing. That was a big part of it, I realize now, the push-me/pull-me aura beaming off all beautiful things. Sexual radar, full blast. That was the thorn on the rose, the crucial wounding detail. Those pictures said: O thrill! O danger! O more-to-know! Still, it got exhausting. This was *me me me,* writ large. It was like those middle-aged emphatically cultured ladies in *The Music Man,* acting out their Keats in River City. *A Grecian Urn,* they had sonorously purred in their circle, arms thrown up, the most earnest exaggerated meaning pasted on their faces.

We were bad. We couldn't help it. We started to laugh but choked it down. This is where Catholic school deep in my gene pool paid off. I could go poker-sober in a second. My old St. Pat's compatriot, that comic genius Deborah Durbin, would have approved. Frances could only turn away; her small convulsions kept on.

She's just really moved, I told Emil. This happens to her a lot.

He nodded. He understood. Naturally. And unfazed, he stared into the photograph at hand with renewed ardor as Frances took a while to settle down, her laughter a kind of weird, fading counterpoint to the room's quiet. What I mean is, in a very few minutes we dropped all that, we came around. Because Emil kept mooning over those pictures of his long-ago wife like some lost Casanova, not really stricken—no second thoughts, he didn't seem to miss her. It was a welling up in appreciation, about her but about himself too, a former world that belonged to both of them. She was part of his universe, after all, if you counted everything. And now Frances and I were somehow included in that count. Still, what got me even then was that beauty itself could be dated, its postures and poses time-bound, sort of *you-had-to-be-there.* What we thought hokey and staged, or out-and-out pretentious, completely smittened him. We were seeing it happen.

So there were fashions, trends, whole strata of fade-in/fade-out judgments concerning this beauty thing. Bodies could change drastically, be *read* so differently. Decades later, watching women's basketball at Purdue, I'd be amazed at such differences again, howbeit in quite another way: the female passion of the players themselves—lithe, quick, unpredictable, and all muscled grace—versus the canned feminine sheen of the cheerleaders on their default setting of singsong shouts and turns, smiling on cue under the flashing shade of their pompoms.

But again, that matter of truth? Old photographs could be deceiving. My grandmother, for instance, who at 8 lost her mother, Sally Gruelle. I have a picture taken shortly after that, 1890 or so, mounted on thick black cardboard as so many of Emil's were. In it, I see four children sadly posed, in center place the oldest girl, Lucy, about 13, with her long curly hair. Next to her, my grandmother as a child, and Lillian, just a year younger, and then her little brother Ivor, at five—all three with cut-to-the-quick boy haircuts, all looking grimly into the future. Their distraught father insisted on taking a scissors to their hair, she told me, the younger ones who couldn't care for themselves that way. She'd fill with rage every time she saw that picture. Oh, that hair! she'd say and fume and carry on. It was years before I'd realize that her anger wasn't embarrassment about how she looked, not humiliation at all. It was grief.

Beauty and truth. Either one could be a little like that clear plastic box in the Lincoln boy-van, a surge of blue water washing to one side, then the other. Just a small thing in your hands but it could, if held close enough, equal *ocean*. Too long in its presence, turning things over and over, you could get vast and dizzy yourself, drown even.

Just *look* at her, Emil kept saying, taking up one stylized picture after another and handing them to us. This one, he'd say. Oh, wait, no—*this* is the one you have to see.

The fact is—Emil White had an eye. He must have been used to sizing up such things, thumbs-up or down. More, I suspect he could look *through* things, into their essence. He himself was a painter, not trained, more in the Grandma Moses tradition of merely picking up a brush one day and going at it, what the hell. An *American Primitive* is what art historians call him now; *Outsider Art* is the phrase in fashion. Because he had—continues to have—a certain fame in that category though he was modest about that, not even the one to mention it, as I recall. It was later that I learned of his reputation, beyond what Frances said at the time.

Emil's an artist. Did you know that? She had turned to me, then gestured to his paintings on the wall, pointing out her favorites. Mostly they were of Big Sur—mountains and highway and the sea done up direct and dreamlike, the way a screwed-up perspective can be thoroughly charming and show how memory works half the time. But he had some town pieces too, all in dazzling blues and reds and yellows and greens. Amazingly, Emil was color blind too. He was proud of that fact, waving it around like a flag. It only means I'll never *fear* color, is what he happily told us.

It only hits me now, *now,* as I write these words: wasn't Ned an artist too? Hadn't Jack told me that once? And that he was always making something odd, beautiful, *out there,* going full blast. That had to be the connection—to Emil White and whatever else. . . . That's it. The collage he'd mostly finished at the Sunderlands. Of course. And even that poor plum tree of song and story in Mill Valley, so colorfully papered and yarned and marshmallowed up before the rains soaked and battered it to myth. Two and two equals—five. Bingo, as Woody liked to say. But I never *saw* that, what was so brilliantly obvious.

Back in that long-ago house, I asked Emil about a city scene up on his wall, with its bent streets and people.

Oh, that was before I learned to make buildings stand up straight, he told us.

59

So Ned had been an artist, of whatever sort. So the roof flies off a house. So the locks fall off doors. That, and the drugs, and the time itself, those years now so hard to imagine where roofs were supposed to do that. And doors themselves routinely walked away from their locks, out of nothing if not pure curiosity. Isn't that how love begins?

This small looming fact about Ned: it changes things, the way the rain above and outside that cave completely altered our sense of where we'd already walked. I think of my brother, years later, when he stood on my porch with his immense box camera, radiant, ready to dive into and under its dark shroud, saying: *sometimes everywhere I look, I see!* I'd put that scene in a locket if I had one. I'd wear it around my neck.

How monstrous and thrilling to see like that. The line between body and world is—where? A moot point, useless and silly to track because it's already vanished into the next thing, and the next thing, and the next.

60

There remained the more earthbound, semi-dicey matter of where we would sleep. I moved in and out of that thought all day and even brought it up to Frances in a private off-moment at Esalen when Emil had edged away from us, and he was standing, at one with—yes—yet another beautiful blond in very little but a beaded vest. She appeared to be snuggling back.

I don't think he'll hit on me, Frances said as we tried to watch those two without appearing to.

Only she didn't say *hit on;* that phrase came into parlance later, I think, and I can't recall when *putting the moves*—or *the make—on* anyone made its appearance in the lexicon of the young. She probably said he wouldn't be *coming on* to her this time around. Whatever way you thought about it, the possibility grew worrisome. Frances figured she was safe, out of the question, given Ned. She was literally beyond reach, thanks to tragedy.

It's too close, you know? she told me. I don't think Emil will try anything.

That was another way to put it: would he *try something?* It was one of those vague phrases my mother used when my brother and I were teenagers. There were others, often involving something she considered *off color,* another puzzling phrase—*ma, what color is that?* She'd point out a remark we'd heard and were starting to repeat as *suggestive.* Which meant no-doubt-about-it, case closed, not allowed. That was our cue to ask with feigned innocence: *suggestive of what, ma? what?* She'd shake her head like forget it, she knew our smart aleck tricks, she was on to us. She wasn't about to be *drawn into* a conversation like that.

I think of it now as an exercise in remote sensing, talking around the point, *suggestive,* at heart an introduction to metaphor, its wiring near electric and quick, the basis of all poetry according to Aristotle. But one could be more direct. In a high school English class my freshman year, our teacher, Sister Mary Ignatius, in an effort to prepare us for the rigors of literary criticism, repeatedly assigned what she called Deep Meaning or simply DM, and asked us to write. That was a form of x-ray vision too, not to mention a nod to the power of image itself.

Give me sixty words on the DM of a leaf, she'd say out of nowhere.

It could be the DM of a blank sheet of paper. Or a thumbtack. Or a shoe. Or a toothpick. She liked it best when a few of us really sucked up and got theological, the thumbtack, for instance, the point that enters the soul *like sin* or the toothpick, a tiny bit of a once mighty tree, just what we can understand of God's endless mercy. These she read aloud with pleasure at the end of the hour while the writer turned color—in pride or embarrassment, depending on the level of cynicism involved.

It was appalling, the predictability of such a brown-nose stunt. But worse, it took planning and a certain willfulness I didn't think quite ethical given the freedom implied by the exercise itself. My efforts were more along the lines of a blank sheet of paper being like snow, a cliché I tried to improve with something about *these words themselves which make their long way through the frozen cold of the endless blank sheet, one dark footprint at a time which the wind will dissolve, fill in with more snow and more snow until the world is a blizzard, impossible to see out there and you keep walking and walking until there's a fence, and then an old rusty swing set and . . .* Cut! Because I was over the word limit by then. Sister Ignatius might read mine to the class but only as an example of what was *not* truly worthy DM since this was merely image opening to further image so it didn't *mean* very much in the end, this *stream-of-consciousness* sort of thing. It was important to focus. And vital to nail it down to a larger issue.

No ideas, girls, that's the problem here, she would have said, though I do see an imagination at work. But I'm afraid *this* writer is just letting herself get carried away.

Wasn't that the point, to get carried away? In fact, we loved the whole notion of DM and at lunch cherished our perverse takes on it, our answer to Sister Sulpice's dating tips, I guess, those ravioli turned into pillows to tempt boys or those designing, dangerous tablecloths, white as bedsheets. That's Catholic school for you. Everything meant something else, the thing itself constantly projecting its shadow on the wall. This spill, this overlay.

Okay, what's the DM of a Kotex? someone would say, peeling back the wax paper on her cheese sandwich. Durbin, you do that one! Or—what's the DM of an ice cream bar? A retainer? A bicycle seat? A vanilla wafer? Our ugly gym uniforms? A jock strap, someone else would say—as a dare. Eventually though, the process wore us down. Impossible to live that way. You'd go nuts in a world with nowhere to look without some equation, some *meaning* dragging behind, no matter how curious or funny or even true. You could never just relax, go oblivious and let things be.

My brother's teenage-boy versions, once he got wind of DM, were entirely single-minded. What's a hot-dog and bun? he fired at me. What's a plug and a wall socket? What's peanut butter and jelly all wrapped up in its Wonder bread? He never got off-track.

It was fairly easy to track Emil's intention. What was the DM of those girls in his yard? Or his way of stroking my arm—or Frances's, for that matter, his gazing into our eyes? The DM of all that exuberant—read *hopeful*—talk of the most marvelous female body?

61

At first, I was uncertain whether Frances, via Ned and his fate, was, in fact, Emil-immune. After supper, she slipped into the bathroom for quite a long time. The faucet in there ran by starts and stops. She was clearly at work washing out a few things, something I needed to do too, in the hope they'd dry overnight. So it was, for the first time, just Emil and me. What's the DM of that sudden uncertain drift you sometimes feel, that weight there, moving under the ribcage and down toward your abdomen? Answer: dread and semi-dread.

Which is to say, Emil was making *advances*—another stock expression, this one borrowed from the military arena, battleground talk. His were serious gestures; even I could see that. Not that I was an expert *advancee.* It usually took something akin to a billboard, no, a nuclear device to alert me that someone might be interested. My wiring was faulty that way but it made things simpler, my being stupid about such matters. Not counting the gorgeous Nikos Stephanopoulos, beau-for-a-night-and-in-theory-only, my first genuine boyfriend (the full-service kind, a friend liked to say) was Jack, the one responsible for my being here at all, having introduced me to Frances. And I was genetically engineered for monogamy, even at the boyfriend level. Still, it didn't seem that citing said *boyfriend* to Emil as reason for a cease and desist would cut much. I'd need another ploy.

Emil was giving me a second tour of the place, this time centering on his bedroom. And his big bed which took up nearly all the space. We stood in the doorway as he wrapped himself around me.

You can sleep here, he said rather sweetly.

Emil, I said, yeah, I could. But—I can't. It took a while to get that out. And without adding the standard *but you're a nice guy and I like you a lot* line of crap either. After all, he could have been my father, my grandfather even. He seemed startled by my refusal but not insulted.

But you must tell me *why* you can't, he finally said. So I can convince you! And before I could speak again, he diligently set himself to that end, murmuring and caressing.

Because. . . . I've taken a vow of chastity, I blurted out, trying discreetly to extract myself from his arms.

I suppose this was akin to my old Jesuitical move in the confessional at St. Eugene's. Because I *had* taken the vow, I told myself, I really had—for *that* particular spot on earth anyway, the promise going into effect about three minutes ago. I could see Emil was still thinking, *reconnoitering,* that this was a highly original take on the subject.

But you have a boyfriend at home, don't you? Poor boyfriend! he nuzzled.

Yes, but I've taken this vow. It's serious, cross-my-heart. I mean it.

And will such a vow be in force when you get back?

This was getting tricky. I'd have to stick to my guns or at least say I would. Luckily Emil had a new thought.

Ah, but you don't need to do *anything,* he said suddenly, coming up for air. You can do nothing to your heart's content and be as chaste as you wish. Just leave it to me. I am strong and hungry! I will do it all!

Decades later, it was an old friend who took me to task on the matter. That sounds too good to be true, she said. The guy was a total love slave! To let it all happen to you? And never have to do a thing? You were out of your mind not to take him up on it. You were *crazy.*

62

Frances and I both slept in the living room that night, she on the couch while I hunkered down on a thin mat under blankets Emil supplied. He stood in the kitchen and said goodnight to us, sad but good-natured. I waved from the floor. Then I was trying *to find my spot* in that makeshift bed, something my grandmother always said one had to do with meticulous care before letting go, sinking down, past dream.

Frances was out in no time, but I couldn't sleep. I imagined this was where Ned had sacked out too, probably right where his wife—no, his widow—lay now though I had the feeling the guy actually never slept. Still, he must have stretched out on that couch, eyes wide open or not. By most accounts, he walked around in a state of permanent undoing and awe.

There were stars. I could see them through the window, more stars than night sky, it seemed. How did humans ever manage to pick out a few, put together the constellations, coherent shape after shape, pictures that might lead to *story*? I remembered the line drawings in an old textbook pretending the exact moment of such invention, ragged boys with sheep looking up at the sky around 2 a.m. and pointing. Why weren't *they* sleeping? Pegasus, the Great Bear, Cassiopeia easing crooked onto her lightning bolt throne. An embarrassment of riches up there, one still the heart

of my favorite joke, that play on the name of a sidekick star: what
did Orion say to his dog? Pause one, two, three: Are you *Sirius*?

Who's awake? the Great Horned Owl sings out all night.

Me too! he answers himself.

63

We were out of there early but not before Emil fixed us eggs and toast and good black tea and we had gathered up our line-dried shirts and underwear from back behind the house. He wanted to talk dreams.

Sorry. I slept right through mine, Frances said. She was cutting toast at a cross angle, the way grown-ups do for kids.

I didn't have much to offer either since mainly, for me, it was dozing all night, my asking myself: had I slept? Or was I sleeping and just dreaming I was awake enough to come up with such an answer? In short, I'd spent the time somewhere in the tiresome passage between states of being, that barely conscious halfway house of near image and not-quite-remembering-it-later.

Emil's dreams were fantastic, he told us. Of women, of course. Non-stop. What a night! he told us. He was exhausted. Where are you headed today? he asked after a second cup of tea. And I looked at Frances too.

Ned went from here to that commune in Colorado, didn't he, Emil?

I think so. He talked about the place, yes, although. . . . Emil trailed off, looked away, then back at her and stayed there.

That was it, I felt sure—they *had* talked, probably at length. And I would never hear the unhappy details.

The place in southwest Colorado, Frances said, it was an old motel or something. She was pinning it down, talking maps and directions, a solid counterforce to the awkward moment. Emil moved toward the small cutting board to make us cheese sandwiches to take. We each got some grapes in a small paper sack, a sign this was really it, our adventure at Big Sur ending.

Well Emil, this has been more than great, Frances said as she rose and did the last fiddling with her pack.

We were both thanking him, and soon headed down the narrow drive, those immense redwoods behind us. But not before Emil was all over us, cuddling and breathing kisses. He had a reasonable reason now. He was saying good-bye.

64

It turned out Frances did have a map, or at least directions. Ned had a relative named Keith at that commune in Colorado, though *relative* was a stretch, really a very distant fourth or fifth cousin come into the family by way of—I don't know—an aunt who married in about fifty years ago, Aunt *So and So,* even the name lost by now. This Keith had filled Frances in earlier, by phone. I don't recall a thing about the ride from Big Sur to that arid, sunny place, only that the landscape surprised me once we got near, so desert-like—not *like,* the real thing including sagebrush and cactus and little bits of stray greenery. Colorado. Wasn't this supposed to be a place of mountains and trees? Maybe that was the northern part of the state.

What I do know is that we left Emil's early on Thursday that week, and when I stare at a map dated 1971, I see a manic spiderweb of roads with mountainy, deserty blanks in it—certainly more than a day's journey. My guess is we went over on 152, picking up Woody's route 5—but taking it south—to 49, up to 89, then east on 160 unto 163, unto who-knows-where-we-actually-traveled, through Nevada again and Utah, and finally into southern Colorado. Maybe route 70 got into it too. In any case, I guess it was an advantage, two young women with their thumbs out, no Woody to chaperone. Because it seems we got there in a flash though it took many hours, and a while between rides. I was mainly sleeping when I ended up in the back seat, so time passed quickly enough. Frances had agreed to taking turns now, chatting up every *other* driver and riding shotgun.

A dark blue Cadillac, massive and ship-like and gleaming, pulled over.

Whoa, said Frances, crossing her fingers. Hey, this might be our last ride too. We're awfully close now.

The front passenger door seemed to open by itself, and slow, which was eerie enough. We hadn't even touched the handle, nor had the driver. We felt a blast of cold, air-conditioned air, a rarity then, the ultimate luxury. Inside: a large, late middle-aged man wearing a business suit. Out here, in freaking nowhere, we'd say to each other later. So early on a Friday too. Definitely peculiar. We'd toy with another idea a little later: maybe he was a UFO guy, or an angel from some cornball movie and we turned up on his must-aid-and-abet list.

Can I help you ladies? He put an equal weight on each word.

Frances mentioned where we were going, what she knew of the address, the nearest crossroad. I forget the name of the commune, which no longer exists, of course. It doesn't even turn up in histories of such places from that time, actually exhaustive studies now, tenure earned because of them. And I've lost the nearest town too.

The driver made a small *hop in* sort of gesture. Then said mostly nothing for what distance we had left, even when I, on front seat duty now, jabbered on about things obvious, at hand: the milky-blue of sky, the darting jackrabbits, the far away rim of mountains, and the unusual heat lately, it still being March, at least that's what people had told us. He finally spoke about the commune. Not exactly though, more the place it once was, which was something, he said. A grand venture built by a shrewd combination of mining and railroad money in the '20s, two fortunes coming together.

You girls have no idea, he told us. You see, those were more sensible days when families married, not man and wife.

He dropped back into silence. I wondered if he had been to the place when he was a kid. Or was connected by blood somehow, turned into a self-made sort of guy since he'd been heir to a ruin. There was a certain after-the-fact melancholy about him.

But scads of people, he began again, would make the long trip in every season. Properly a resort, believe me. Thousands, year-round. Because the hot springs brought everyone here. They had a pool.

I tried to superimpose those gad-abouts of the *Gatsby* era out there on the desert, in its heat and cold by turns, its dry air, what-the-hell hardened party types tooling about in their roadsters, women in ultra chic bucket hats and short skirts and cigarette holders, men in their fedoras and sullen wisecracks. And given the fact of the hot springs, I added long-legged striped bathing suits to the scene as they stepped demurely into those waters.

Then the Depression, he said. Almost did the place in. Terrible. And he shook his head. I mean terrible.

He was speaking completely in starts and stops now, with longer than usual pauses between, a way of talking that forced you to nod at each empty space.

But, he continued. It limped along. Past the war years. Before the trains quit. Before it was city city city where people wanted to go. Then. Well. They chucked the thing. Abandoned. They just. Walked away.

Was any of this true? Sad and heroic and big as history: it all leaked out of the guy himself, in what he said and pointedly didn't say, those pauses. He was watching himself tell it, I realized, fully moved by his own eloquence. Through the windshield, I was witness to remarkable stuff *right here, right now*—for starters, a roadrunner, I think, moving quickly beyond my side vision, like something right out the cartoons. A visitation, of sorts. But I didn't dare interrupt.

Out here, who can make it really? the driver said. It seemed a question addressed to sky, mountains, that roadrunner equally— and to Frances, to me.

With that, he made a dramatic stop, spinning the car completely around to head back where he came from. He'd gone impossibly out of his way to bring us here.

Ladies, he bowed, his words coming slowly, like he was taking a snapshot of each one: the pleasure was all mine. And he pointed up, to the left where the main buildings and everything behind them stood back from the road.

This time both doors did open, all by themselves.

65

It was an honest-to-god 1960s commune, howbeit sprung from someone's dream of luxury in the '20s. Pink, for one thing, and made of stone with all sorts of intricate scrolling worked into the door lintels or wherever there happened to be a column. Or maybe I'm making that up. I saw the standard double row of motel units same as you find now, only each seemed a ghost of itself too. That could have been the whirlpool of dust rising up now and then: atmosphere. The kind they'd pay a lot for, if this were a movie. But the entire place seemed something out of a film—*on location,* like the ghost town in an easterner's—or any midwesterner's—notion of the old wild west, the kind where all the buildings creak and sway, each door hanging crooked, one jamb intact, where the sun is always going down and there's perennial twilight. But not entirely. The place looked semi-cared for, and functioning.

So this was the last spot Ned had been. That fact was quietly sobering again, like this was some sort of shrine, and we'd be purified, or at least something in Frances's head would click shut or open. It was midmorning; we'd driven all day and night, sleeping on and off in various cars to get here. No one in sight now. There weren't even voices.

Frances, are you sure this is the right commune, the one Ned was at? I said.

We were headed toward what appeared to be the main building, more scrolly stonework on the door frames and windows, an arched canopy sort of thing built onto it, inviting anyone in.

They're here, don't worry. I called, remember? That guy Keith told me it would be okay to come. Besides, he gave me specific instructions. I swear this is it. Drop it, would you? You're freaking me out.

I don't recall who finally welcomed us, Keith or someone else, but there *were* people there. Frances was right. But only partly so. There'd been a big argument a day before we arrived so half— more than half—of the commune had gone off in a huff.

As was the custom in those days, I want to say.

66

Inside the main house where the office once was, they showed us the kitchen, the big common room, the array of other, smaller spaces, one a kind of library now, they said—books people on the move had left there, or titles found on the library *take-it, it's free* cart or discovered at rummage sales. I almost gave them the novel Jack urged me to bring along; I hadn't cracked a page. I do remember picking up Aldous Huxley's odd little book, *The Art of Seeing,* on altering your vision. Not *vision* in the grand sense, merely the cornea/iris/pupil kind, clever ways to train yourself out of glasses and into the brave new world of 20/20. It amused me, how practical it was, complete with exhaustive eye exercises. And also the fact that some people might well reach for the book—as I did—thinking *transcendental,* thinking *mind fuck*—and get a sudden optometry lesson instead. That was itself a lesson. I thought of those long moments in any eye exam, in the twilight of such an office, the guy sliding circles of glass to get the truest moment of not-blur among so much blurring: is this one better? Or this one? How about this one? Until the difference is so close you almost panic, can't even imagine an accurate answer.

And the fight that happened before we arrived? Everyone was obsessed with it though I don't recall, if I ever knew, what the fray had been about. At a general meeting—these happened weekly—

someone got pissed, then a surge kicked up, a dark wave, a whole high tide of anger about how things were run at the commune, who got to do—or had to do—this thing or that. I don't know how many people packed up and took off still furious, but apparently a lot. They promptly took the bus off the place, the commune's bus, threatening to make it all the way to Mexico.

Our bus. It belongs here, god damn it, to every single one of us, said a large woman, her long hair hidden behind a tightly knotted paisley headscarf. Fuck that noise, she added.

I could imagine such a bus, some old third-hand school junker lovingly repaired, painted over in DayGlo with words like *Joy* and *Peace* in large letters on the side, big red and yellow wiggly lines on the roof. Then someone had, no doubt, hand-brushed that black and white symbol—the ying and yang cuddled famously together—above the tailpipe.

Frances and I listened, trying to look sympathetic. We made worried and/or outraged little noises, not even words, designed on the spot to show solidarity. Of course we took their side since they were our hosts and they were stuck with us, as guests.

It was one bad trip, the former Keith-in-waiting said. No shit, man. Bad upon bad.

He shook his head, reliving the argument, I could see that. He was watching them peel out of the lot in a cloud of gravel and dust again too, the movie on replay, not one person aboard waving good-bye. He had walked us over to one of those little motel-like units where we were to stay the night.

You guys can use these digs. They belong to Unicorn but she's with them. And not coming back any way soon, I guess.

He opened the door and we saw the room done up in what looked like elaborate spider webbing, baseboard to ceiling, a mattress with an Indian bedspread on the floor squeezed in under and into all that hanging yarn and wire, center stage. There were hundreds of unlit candles and the overwhelming scent of patchouli. We stood still for a moment, staring.

Well, maybe not, he said. No room to even breathe in here. Not for two of you. I have a better idea.

And he ushered us to another unit, three doors down, one with two twin beds, a couple of old blankets, an overhead light, a wobbly broken table by the window. Clearly, no one had lived there for long, ever.

This one's empty enough, he said.

67

It's impossible to know what ordinary life on the commune was like when it was in full swing given the exodus of so many of its citizens. When Frances and I loitered about, and caught any of the handful of people remaining, they seemed overwhelmed— too much to do, with so few on board—or listless, like who-gives- a-shit-now-that-those-slackers/know-it-alls/half-asses-are-gone. Still, people were cutting up vegetables for supper in a few hours, others were lugging water to the garden by the bucketful. We heard about their attempt at a windmill, about the start/stop electric surges that came from it. Know anything about plumb- ing? someone asked me with a hope that didn't last long. For my part, I had a million questions about Ned—who hadn't been mentioned yet that I could tell—but felt that was Frances's place to ask. Anyway, there was still a lot of anger blocking any con- versation; a kind of grief cloud hovered everywhere, given the dramatic departure of their friends.

Bad vibes, said a tall guy in beaded everything and patches on his patches. He had this wannabe mohawk too, before I remem- ber there being such a thing outside of the pen-and-ink drawings in history books though he probably wasn't the first white guy in twentieth-century America to have one.

We got to go on without them, he said, that's all. And do what we gotta do.

He sounded like a despondent basketball coach who's always talking about *taking care of the basketball* like it was a simple but hopeless matter. Then he noticed me staring at his hair.

I'm into the Sioux. Like, but you're really supposed to call them the Dakotas. That's what they called themselves. *Sioux*'s a fucking white man name.

So they had haircuts like that?

This? No, this is Iroquois, man. I studied the stuff. But I like this look. Even though that was one hard-ass tribe. Their clubs and shit. Their knives and spears and that. Bloody. They were into fighting in a big way, and there was always something going on. But I'm for peace, man. You know what I mean? Hey, I marched on Washington last year. A lot of us here did.

I could instantly picture that bus filled to the brim, this guy with his after-or-before-its-time mohawk and everyone hard at work on their picket signs as they pulled into the city, headed toward the reflecting pool. Suddenly I saw everyone else we'd met on this trip. A curious hallucination. The Lincoln boys going wacko with envy just at the mention of the march. They'd start sniffing around for details to show they'd been there all along, maybe on that very bus. And outside, in that city for real, there'd be a prim, well-dressed Joyce Sunderland looking out her office window that moment too, or taking her lunch break, walking back down 17th Street in her perfectly matched outfit, tisk tisk tisking the wild hippies from out of town in their stupid bus. Above them, Satamanyu would be astral-hovering, smiling vacantly in pure joy while someone below, already *on the bus* would be honked off all over again remembering that chicken leg in his icebox. And Emil While would be there, I know it, color blind as he claimed he was, doing the whole hip mangled thing up right, in bright yellow and green and blue, putting himself in somewhere, a tiny presence in the corner, like in those ancient Chinese scrolls.

But where was Ned? What would be the DM of Ned? Sleeping—or stretched out larger than life, at the very bottom of it all, about to enter a most marvelous dream, like my favorite among all of my favorites of Chagall's sick-to-death-no!-turned-complete-love-of-this-world paintings.

I was losing it, letting all the scenes of the week swim together in some glittering muddy pool. Memory. Even then, it was getting too crowded in there.

68

So I was napping in our little two-bed unit, probably most of the afternoon. I hoped that would help, a sweet long doze. Then Frances was shaking me, her hand on my shoulder.

Hey. Wake up!

Huh?

Hey listen, this is super cool. We're going swimming! In that hot springs pool they have.

Hot springs? What?

You know, the one the Cadillac guy told us about when this place was an old resort? It's still here.

I was sitting up now, trying to click in again, where I was—check, Colorado—and who she was—Frances, yes—and why I was even here.

Swimming? I said. Like in a swimming pool? Uh, Frances, I don't think I can. I didn't bring my bathing suit. She looked at me closely.

We don't *need* bathing suits. She said it pointedly, like this was blocks for the blind, obvious, a non-issue.

I took this in, trying to figure. Given Esalen, and our near-miss in the baths there, I don't know why it would have been such shocking news.

What do you mean? You mean. . . .

Yes. You got it. *Bingo!* she said, quoting Woody, that's what I mean. Time to mellow out!

But I don't even *know* these people.

Hey, no one gives a damn about that here. Come on. There's hardly any people anyway. Considering, I mean. There could have been a ton more out there. But you know, they're in friggin' Mexico now. Anyway, I heard it's *weird* water in that pool. I mean, once you get in, no one can spot a thing. It's murky and hot and not at all see-through or anything.

I don't know. This is a big one for me, Frances. It really is.

Yeah, well. So what!—no offense. Come on. You said you were a *lapsed* Catholic, right? How lapsed can you get? Anyway, you *have* to come with me. You really do. Right now too, before supper. That's when they said.

69

It took a few minutes, my mulling and remulling this over, something I never had to do very long at Big Sur where the crowds in those Esalen baths saved me the trouble. Had I a time machine, I might have whizzed off to the future again, to our first days at Netherwood Co-op when my husband and I would be asked to attend the membership meeting where Mr. Ts'ou was getting grilled, his initial interview in the long process of joining the house. Really it was my husband David they wanted at the meeting, given his grasp of Chinese. He would be handy as a translator, if things got confusing.

Netherwood was famous for its "clothing optional" rule. And in those days, enough dope smoking went on in that place as anywhere else too. The current members needed to make sure this guy from China and so much older, almost 50, knew these things, that he wouldn't be shocked at the casual nudity in the house or any random toking up that went on. Netherwood's meetings were weekly, but this was a special one. All decisions required full consensus—that was sacred—meaning everyone present had to agree. None of that "majority rule" stuff. Sometimes this took hours, down to the last browbeating of one errant opinion holder though sometimes that person simply wouldn't budge. Then the motion—or whatever the key point of such a long, late-evening discussion—failed and everyone finally went to bed.

Mr. Ts'ou sat rigidly at the edge of a chair in his white buttoned-to-the-top shirt and black pants, his hands placed on his knees like he was about to be shot from a cannon. They were trying to explain Netherwood's place in the proud history of Madison Co-ops, how it was different, how it had real style, how it was the best and definitely the hippest. It was all those things, no question, set wonderfully right on Lake Mendota, a three-story, gorgeous 1920s rococo mansion with surprising, austere touches—heavy little-paned medieval windows that opened out to the lake, serious woodwork that edged the tall ceiling where it met each wall. A classy joint, as that aging hippie lady in *San Fran* had said when she got wind of the Sunderland's neighborhood. Must be partly the water thing, just the thought of being close to any kind of shore. It upped the ante.

Now, Joe, here's the thing, Seeker was saying as he threw back his blond dreadlocks in a great sweep. We have this *other* house policy. See, we sometimes smoke dope here. No biggie. Is that okay with you?

Mr. Ts'ou turned to us with a quizzical look. And David translated Seeker's remarks into something close enough. Later, he told me he hadn't known the Chinese word for "marijuana"; he had to substitute with *people here enjoy opium-like substances.*

Mr. Ts'ou bent his head to the side. Ah, he said, with a little intake of breath.

And one more thing, Joe, said the beautiful Nancy-turned-Starfish in an airy sort of way. Some of us, well, a few of us walk around naked in the house sometimes. When it strikes us, you know. We just go with it. That cool with you?

He turned again to us for a clue. This one had been easier, David told me. The Chinese he managed now was simple: *some of these people do not wear clothes.* But that intelligence took a minute to settle. Mr. Ts'ou stared out the big window of that room, out to the lake where it emphatically continued to be late summer, where sailboats cut through a hazy blue expanse. Finally he turned back to us.

It is all right, he said slowly and distinctly in English. I have studied American culture.

70

Of course, this dropping trou thing wasn't any *regular* in-your-face walk-around habit I knew of in the country, not in the Midwest or out west either, not even at Esalen, where it was traced back, in theory at least, to simple bathing, once the only spot on that desolate stretch of coast to manage such a thing. And although taking off one's clothes was the whole point at *nudist* colonies, that was hardly the general scheme of things in America, even in the '60s though all those books now about hippies and free love would have you believe otherwise. Mostly, people are private, and certainly then as awkward and self-conscious as they are now about such things.

There *was* that bad-boy, throw-it-all-to-the wind impulse—that must have been part of the kick at Netherwood. Slipping out of one's clothes was more common near water, I suppose, what kids might try in a sleepy Norman Rockwell sort of river, or how drunken teenagers take a dare at midnight in some abandoned quarry, never letting on to their mothers. Swinging out of trees on ropes could be involved, and serious, thrill-a-minute shrieking, in either vignette. And it was routine then, I'm told, that troops of boy scouts rarely bothered with bathing suits in secluded places, once a habit at most YMCAs too, in their all-guy swimming pools. A name had evolved to cover some of that. What is it about language? It helped, as usual, to have a category—a tidy, seemingly harmless box to put it in. That's all we'd be doing, I told myself: *skinny-dipping.* Sort of.

It's your decision. But I'm going to the john now, said Frances, abruptly laying down the gauntlet like a schoolmarm. When I come out, I hope you'll be walking over there with me.

71

When we got to the main building, which opened into a kind of roofed plaza where the swimming pool had been set in the ground long ago, three or four people were already stripped down and either going into the water, or had just emerged. The sun well on its way out, lanterns were ready to rip, and candles had been left on various tables. It was late, already near twilight.

I stared at the pool—a small, crumbly rectangle. I don't recall all that much more except Frances was right, the water did look strange. Viscous. Like I'm told everything gels at the back of an eye, grayish or bluish in there and the threat is it could all go rigid and break away. But when someone eased into the pool, it rocked and waved as any self-respecting seasick-making element might. Frances was looking around for a place to take off her clothes.

Well, okay then, she said. And in a second, slipped out of her T-shirt, her jeans and stood for a couple of breaths, almost as thin as Twiggy, that icon of our adolescence that Ned had included in the Sunderland's collage. Then Frances lowered herself off the side, into that drink.

The warmest drink imaginable, it turns out. I was even quicker, out of my clothes in a half-second to her second and into the pool. I was standing up, *and* floating. But it sure wasn't ordinary water, so warm and thick you sank and buoyed up, sank and steadied, turned over and over by its soft billows as you rose up again and again, suspended. I radiated with it, the heat coming though me, impossible slur of yes and more yes.

Again, hadn't Frances been right? Who cared what anyone looked like? Who the hell was looking? O my god, I said out loud to no one. She was bounding under and over her own delicious warm wave. This place *was* something—still! I might have insisted to our driver, the guy in his big Cadillac who had lamented its fate. Fate: meaning it long ago disappeared. But wasn't this water the very heart and soul of the place *right now*? Here we were, sucked down into its jaws, unbelievably soothed. It swallowed us. Comfort: all trouble back to one instant of losing then finding some other marvelous way out of, or back into.

After a while, someone spoke to me. I swear there were words, distant, and closer. Then it was so quiet. Then more than one of them shouting—what? I couldn't hear. Were they saying come out? Oh sweet never ever, no way! This was wonderful. O my god. I was *never* getting out, thank you. Thank you very much. Very much. So very much.

I caught Frances's voice. *You have to come out! You've got to!* But did I owe her? Or anyone? Oh, this was lovely. I was adrift and it was dark and it was. . . .

Someone had my arm, and there were other hands on my right leg. They were pulling me from the water, telling me I had to, I did, it was dangerous to be in there that long. All the life sucked out of me or was it you or was it me again, collapsing.

I tried to stand on the concrete, the stone, the patio. How could I stand? I wanted back to those warm waves, that embrace and how endless. But the awful weight of everything now—the air a thousand pounds on me, me—melted to nothing, crawling naked, with nothing on, nothing. I couldn't care less except I was cold, I was caving in, barely making it to the table, this hand and then this other hand, this knee, right, then left. Someone was wrapping me in a towel, maybe a sheet. Oh *moment of history,* be specific and huge, remember this gesture, whatever shimmering word. Someone was telling me to breathe slowly and deep and giving me water. Someone was saying *lie down, you have to.* Someone was saying *drink more of this, nice and cool. Please.*

72

When I came to, came *back* to myself from wherever I'd been, I felt a pillow under my head and a blanket around me. I looked up into the lantern-lit dark and people were eating. They were shiny in that light. They were laughing and talking. I raised up on one arm and—my clothes? Where were my clothes? I had everything once; I had a T-shirt. Then Frances was at my ear and telling me. And I was putting on that shirt. I was slipping back into my jeans.

You still need to stay here—pretty much flat, I mean—for a while, she said. You got dehydrated or something. It's heavy shit, what happened to you. That's what they said. You really freaked us out, you know that?

Okay, I said, and leaned back again. Through the cracks in the overhang, I saw a few stars but it was cloudy.

Here, I think you can try this. The mohawk guy had joined us, a plate in his hand. Man, that was bad. But you're probably hungry, right?

What are those? I said. I saw homemade bread cut into squares with a greenish something-or-other smeared all over them, a few with a tomato slice, most going solo.

Avocado sandwiches. Made 'em myself, man. Here, take one. They're good-eating.

I had noticed avocadoes, of course, green and all sizes in the postcards I'd seen when we entered California. Surreal, that they actually grew on trees, shiny and the color of leaves themselves. Leathery, I thought later, finding them in various markets, just so in their post-orchard afterlife, like something you'd take into a shoe repair place in some last ditch effort, though this delicate green stuff must be what lay *inside* that crinkled black hide of the thing. But to *eat* one. I don't know. Still, I reached for the plate. And took one. And another, and another—a little bland. But not bad, I liked the texture.

Uh, Frances, I said after a few minutes. Listen, I don't feel so hot right now.

And no, I definitely did not. It all came back up, right there, in front of everyone. I'd never feel sicker—or more embarrassed.

How many years before I'd eat another avocado? Too many to count.

73

I was really sleeping it off then. All night, and into the next morning. I woke alone in that little room. It looked like Frances hadn't used the other bed at all. I felt way better. I washed up and changed into my last clean clothes—underwear, T-shirt. Now I really *was* hungry.

Should I be worrying about Frances? Earlier, the day before, having been given this room, we were settling in, she lying on one of the beds. Thin, like Twiggy—I mentioned that before—but she was telling me she liked her hipbones protruding that way, the skin cool and taut there, so all-together, and how glad she was for them.

It's great when you're balling, you know? she said. I love how my bones fit with his bones then, whoever it is, just the feel of that.

It would have shocked me, such private talk, if she wasn't so offhand, so joyful about it. Or maybe it was the joy itself that jolted me because something was changing.

Now she was elsewhere. And probably with—maybe Keith, the cousin so distant he wasn't even a cousin, or maybe someone else. *That* startled me, as fixed as I was on Ned, on finding out *about* Ned, the single-minded purity of that mission. But Frances. . . . He must have become more and more a ghost to her, this handful of days adding endlessly to the count of how long he'd been gone, giving reason and substance. *Gone,* a euphemism of the first order. We were following a track of bread crumbs.

I have to face it, you know? she told me on one of those ramps in southern Nevada. I mean sooner or later. No matter what I find out about Ned, I'm still a fucking widow, right? I'll be that forever! He's not here. And won't be coming back. He just won't. Never. Never. Never.

Yeah, I said. What to tell her then? What to even *imagine* telling her?

Ned's not fucking here anymore! She yelled once, then about three or four times into that sweep of rock and sunset, of hot wind and echoy eerie world upon world out there.

74

I found Frances sipping tea in the main building, finishing the oats Keith had cooked for her, and for anyone who wanted a bowl, I guess.

Like some? he asked. I did. I really did. It occurred to me to say something about last night, my terrible upchuck, spilling my guts—or *tossing my cookies* as we called it when I was a kid. How sorry I was, all that. But no one seemed to care. They either shrugged or changed the subject. I wondered who had cleaned it up and felt shame come back, red and warm, all over again.

Too bad you have to leave today, Keith said, his eyes fixed on Frances. He leaned over to touch her cheek and she leaned into his hand, sweetly, with the slightest tilt to her head.

I was getting my nerve up—why not? It was none of my business, but this was my last chance.

Keith, I said. Ned was here, right? He stayed here—for how long? Before the. . . .

Crack up? he said. Before that, you mean?

He looked at Frances again, and she gave him some sign like *what the hell, you can tell her.* I knew then they had talked all night about it, had pulled all the thorny bits about Ned through a knothole as they slept, or didn't sleep.

Yeah, sure. Of course before that, I said. Because this was where he stayed last, right? And his car—wasn't that *your* car? From this place?

Keith glanced around the table then, at the four or five people there. They all took on a serious-weather look, like a tornado had been mentioned, an earthquake in some distant sad place or a flood there with hundreds missing.

Yes to all of that, Keith said. And yeah, he was 100 percent fucked up when he got here.

That sounded just like Kevin. I looked over at Frances but she was nodding.

Fucked up in a very big way, he added—and more alive than I'd ever seen him.

I figured the *alive* part was mainly due to Emil since Ned had just come from Big Sur. I could picture Emil cooking for Ned, seeing that he had a good hot soaking down at Esalen, their talk cryptic and soothing by turns, about women and whether to keep the buildings in a painting upright or not, and Emil's favorite bird, the red-tailed hawk. But the fucked up part—who knows?

Keith speaks the truth, man, said an older guy at the table in his ponytail and black bushy beard. I'm here to tell you: that stuff Ned was saying, it fucking blew our heads off.

I almost said *like what stuff?* but realized Frances had probably heard all about it the night before. Anyway, it would be a broken record, a repeat of what those Mill Valley guys had said: Ned as mystic, as soothsayer, as witness to the genuine important matters in this life.

Frances, look, I need to show you something, Keith said, now that it's daylight. It might explain a lot, I don't know. He paused, then turned toward me.

You. You come too, if you want.

75

They had this cool old truck on that commune, circa 1958 or so. A Ford, with those wide ripped up seats, duct tape holding them together, and a spider-like stick shift, wobbly, straight up from the floor. We walked out and climbed in, the three of us. Keith and Frances and me.

I have to warn you, Keith said. Like I told you, Frances, Ned had been here for a few days, talking non-stop through his brilliant craziness. We didn't quite know what to do with him after a while, how to help him figure it all. To tell you the truth, he was scaring us, even the hardcore trippers here who know that shit, inside out.

The truck was grinding and coughing. Keith had to keep shifting down, then up again, hammering the clutch. He was practically shouting over it.

Just in time I remembered what Ned always liked best, he was saying. It turns out we had these old buckets of paint in one of the outbuildings. Almost a hundred, I think. Who knows what colors—they came with the place, and dated from when? the early '60s? the '50s? Before that even. The ones that haven't dried out to the bone, just stir those suckers, I told him. Just get a stick in and see what colors they turn into. Whatever you want to do, man. You're the boss.

I bet he loved that, Frances said softly.

We were bumping over ruts you wouldn't believe. Her whispers were half-shouts but came across as quiet, barely out there for us to hear. More like she was talking to herself, and maybe she was. And we had overheard.

Like, we have a decent ladder, tall enough. And I gave him a couple of brushes I had, Keith went on loudly. One big one, he said, one smaller too but nothing tiny like a real artist would use on a canvas or anything. They were brushes a housepainter would pull out of his box of stuff and soak later, in a bucket of turpentine.

We were rounding a corner then, a big barn-like building. Clearly there was more to this place than a pleasure dome from the old days. Real work had gone on at some point—serious farming, and the fixing of small and large annoyingly breakable machines. Maybe there had been animals to tend. Now these guys had similar plans.

Well, here's what I mean, Keith said. Here's what you have to see, Frances.

He pulled up, shifting down until the engine went dead.

76

We sat in the truck a few minutes, the three of us on that wide seat. No one made a sound.

The side of the barn was covered in all manner of paint, high and low, left to right. For starters, your standard mandala, your ying/yang symbol, even a little peace sign at the right lower edge. But the other images: all sizes of faces caught in horror or ecstasy, sorrow or joy but mostly it was pain in those eyes, and every one looking straight out and into us. To be fair, there were bright, Emil-like attempts at landscape or seascape: *amber waves of grain,* and foamy breakers crashing on whatever shore you might imagine, high mountains with winding roads traced into their woods, cactus spotting a desert.

But all was cut and overlaid with cubist body parts—arms, legs, awful eyes and ears and mouths floating by themselves. A cornucopia of styles, layer upon layer, that never seemed to quit. Tiny cars wove in and out, cartoonish but not cute, the driver always Ned hunched over the wheel, his eyes closed half the time, that red hair flying up and out and behind. In one of those cars, the hair kept going, out the window and into a long somehow dire swirling that circled the faces and crept under the seasick waves and up the brown-black rock wall of the canyons. That *swirl* business was a stock visual gesture of the period, usually cheerful enough. But not here.

I would like to say a comforting little house stood in the corner to ground it and, as in one of Emil's pictures, an upright figure happily painted there, that through a window you could see the easel and the can of brushes, that artist himself emphatically mid-stroke. No luck. Instead large animals roamed the side of that barn, invented from various mismatched parts—random wings and hooves, yellowed teeth and claws, front legs and back legs, the many-eyed antennaed eyes of insects that would freeze you instantly if blown-up and close. But they were that big; you couldn't look away. Unthinkable, unnerving creatures, misaligned and wounded, sometimes bloody.

Keith and I understood this much: Frances would have to be the first to speak. So we waited. But she bolted over me, out the passenger door. And began to run.

Let her go, Keith said to me.

77

And that's pretty much what I have of this story I've been waiting thirty-seven years to tell. But a friend was bothered: why now? At the most basic level, I suppose it's only now that I have the writerly nerve to attempt it at all, the patience—and the distance finally—to see it *unfold* again. But there's more. A small moment came later when I lived alone the year after college, working in Hyde Park, in Chicago, at the university library there. I remember Jimmy's—James Wilson's Woodland Tap—and an old guy whose neighborhood bookstore was going under, who would come to drink at that bar every night. Once he said: you know, I get here. I have a shot. I look around, and it hits me—all my friends are dead! How do you imagine that happened? It seemed less melodrama than fact, more poignant than funny though I was in my 20s, still officially immortal and thus immune.

Which is to say: *time*—you can't trust it. And memory itself is a ticking clock. It passes, passes *into.* And maybe, at best, its flashes are only *recovered,* a useful idea since remembering seems a matter of patching and bringing up out of dark, more like fog lifting, some details soaked by rain and unimaginable before. But to follow for those nine days the radiant stain of a ghost: I see that trip west as one of the great privileges of my life. And, more urgently, that Ned *was* an artist, meaning that he made himself a conduit: how he stood between worlds, each so wildly at odds about him—that thought still rattles me, gives off tension and light. The need for poetry begins in that light.

It's possible the shape of Ned's story is too familiar. Does that make it more or less tragic? Ginsberg caught it over a decade earlier: *I have seen the best minds of my generation/ destroyed by madness, starving, hysterical, naked. . . .* Those lines from *Howl* have become a mantra. They inflate to high drama, which may or may not make sense in Ned's case. I just don't know.

Still, this whole thing gets stranger. Another friend recently reminded me how Willa Cather nailed it: we write to recover our lives and maybe mostly our youth. But it reaches beyond that too—less personal, more compelling—when you feel part of a time, a place. The lost late '60s, early '70s gained in urgency for me as I wrote this: to do halfway justice to an era, to be a credible witness though *not* from the lively peace-love-headband-beads center of it all. Like so many in my generation could say: *I just happened to be there,* however I hung back because of age or temperament. And now, it amazes me: the sweet brief nothing-at-all at the start of any life. To remember that, to savor that too, this thing so troublesome when you're first going through it. Time past and time passing. The old bookseller was right: how *do* we imagine that happens?

And human love. The friend who asked *why now?* when he read this story was certain: no, love couldn't save Ned. I disagree. It might have, however momentary. *I Am a Stranger Here Myself,* Emil White called not one but four of his paintings though each swims wildly in its zillion glad colors. Ned was driving home, after all. Who knows what goes on in a car still moving, middle of a continent, that delicate, powerful suspension between past and future? As for Emil's house, *almost* swallowed up by raging wildfires thirty-seven summers later, in 2008: those flames stopped literally at the doorstep, the place spared, still miraculously intact.

For our part, Frances and I got back without incident, hitching straight to Illinois, she to DeKalb, and me going south at some point to Champaign, headed to class that Monday, not missing a word. I returned with the same amount of money I left with: ten dollars. That continues to be startling, the world's generosity to us. And I know we were in some important way protected by our innocence. We had slipped through a keyhole. Partly that was the era. You could do that.

I recall another version of that final morning on the commune. Maybe it's truer to what really happened, I'm not sure. In that memory, Keith and Frances and I walk to the barn and round the corner. And see roughly the same thing—the inside of Ned's head, I called it after that. His demons, to *not* coin a phrase. In that take, Frances looks up and into the painting for a long time. We all do. And are equally locked there. Finally I hear her say: *that's it. I'm done.*

And we were. We hitched out of there within the hour.

Still, I do remember and cherish that truck. I'll keep us sitting there in the cab of the thing staring, probably forever, *up* and *into*. I suppose it doesn't matter. Ned gets huge; he drifts in any case, then begins slowly to vanish. Was it an accident or a suicide? That question never came up; it's only this year that it even occurred to me.

I've changed the names of the living here, but I never saw Woody or Frances again. Jack and I hung on for a little longer, on and off. The last I heard from Frances came in a letter. I was standing in the yard of the place I had rented with some friends the following fall—309 we still call it since that's where it was on Clark before they bulldozed it. The mailman showed up with that note from Frances, forwarded from Della Crooks' boarding house on Green Street. I turned the envelope over. In disbelief— I need to say that. *Mr. Postman,* she had scrawled in red pencil, *Jesus loves you.* But such a moment—this too was *of that time and of that place.*

I've met someone! she wrote in the letter.

He was sweet, he was a Jesus freak. Frances lived with a bunch of them now, in a large apartment above a bowling alley. Standing there, I read again what she had written: for the first time she was really happy. She would pray for me.

Notes and Acknowledgments

To time travel back, one seeks out ways to trigger memory, to relive what's been lost. I was helped first through the obvious sources—road maps from the period and historical studies as well as various periodicals from those years—*Life* magazine, *Newsweek,* and *Time.* I discovered Joanne Fenton Humphrey's book about Emil White and his painting, *Emil White of Big Sur* (Windjammer Adventure Publishing, 1997), a wonderful record, and some of the things Emil told us in 1971, down to the exact phrasing, are echoed in the interviews there. (We obviously weren't the last to hear such comments. Not a surprise, I suppose; his was a radiant and repeatable repertoire.) Jeffrey Kripal's book *Esalen: America and the Religion of No Religion* (University of Chicago Press, 2007) is a solid history of the place and confirmed many things I learned on the visit to Big Sur. I thank Magnus Toren, of the Henry Miller Library, for more detail about Emil White's house. I thank Timothy Miller too, whose *The 60s Communes: Hippies and Beyond* (Syracuse University Press, 1999) helped me grasp the context of my experience in Colorado, though the place Frances and I stayed seems to have been swept away without a trace. His generous response to my e-mails only confirmed this sad fact. And speaking of sad fact: my epigraph from Hans Barth, a German expatriate who died in Rome, pre-translation, is *Wir alle sind Pilger und Fremde,* as elegant and ancient as that city itself.

Enormous gratitude goes to my first readers—of course David and Will Dunlap, who saw versions of the manuscript from the start and made countless suggestions, Will's good eye as to character and scene a particular help. Fiction-writing friends Susan Neville, Jane Hamilton, and Charles Baxter—who either read everything or endured my reading *to* them parts of the book-in-progress—vastly aided me, a poet thrashing about in the brave new waters of narrative prose. Warm thanks go to Joan Swerdloff, Mary Niepokuj, Wendy Flory, Irwin Weiser, Abby Brogden and JoAnn Johnson, Berkeley and Tom McChesney, and Palmira Brummett, my oldest friend, from high school, who responded to this work most usefully. Pat Deflaun, Joseph Kantner, and Cathleen Williams all helped me recall the literal lay of the land in northern California. I appreciate Porter Shreve and Bich Nguyen giving me leads on background sources for the period—Todd Gitlin's thorough *The Sixties: Years of Hope, Days of Rage* (Bantam Books, 1993) or the curious *Hippie Dictionary* (Top Speed Press, 2002) for instance—and for their thoughts, especially Bich's, about writing creative non-fiction in the first place.

The quoted lines of poetry here are from the following collections: *The Collected Poems* by Louis MacNeice (Faber and Faber, 2002); *Blake's Complete Writings,* edited by Geoffrey Keynes (Oxford University Press, 1971); *The Carrier of Ladders,* by W. S. Merwin (Atheneum, 1973), and *Collected Poems: 1947–1980* by Allen Ginsberg (Harper, 1984). The two songs whose few fragments I quote are "Eve of Destruction," composed by P. F. Sloan in 1965, and "I Should Have Known Better," by Lennon and McCartney from *A Hard Day's Night*, 1964. Many thanks to Blake scholar Jim Watt for his locating—pretty much instantly— the lines in my head from *The Marriage of Heaven and Hell* I was trying to find in print.

Excerpts from this memoir, slightly altered to be a bit more free-standing, have appeared in *The Massachusetts Review, Prairie Schooner, Ninth Letter,* and *The New England Review.*

This book was revised—tweaked and added to and subtracted from—at my home in West Lafayette, Indiana. But the initial full draft was written in two most treasured places—the first half at the MacDowell Colony and the second at the Anderson Center in Red Wing, Minnesota. To go back, to *see* these years again, totally absorbed and challenged me: both places gave me courage.

MARIANNE BORUCH is the author of seven poetry collections, most recently *The Book of Hours* and *Grace, Fallen from,* and two books of essays, *Poetry's Old Air* and *In the Blue Pharmacy.* Her awards include Guggenheim and NEA fellowships, and residencies from the Rockefeller Foundation's Bellagio Center and Isle Royale National Park. Her poems and essays have appeared in the *New Yorker, Poetry,* the *Nation, Paris Review, Field, Ploughshares, Georgia Review, Poetry London, Yale Review,* and elsewhere. She developed Purdue University's MFA Program in English, serving as its first director from 1987 to 2005, and remains on its faculty. Since 1988, she has also taught at Warren Wilson College's low-residency Program for Writers. She and her husband live in West Lafayette, Indiana.